The Grid:

Lessons
from the
Men of
Grindr

LEX, ESQ.

DEDICATION

To all of my friends. Your unwavering support is what motivates me. To Jazzmyn, Elisabeth, and Alisa, for your selflessness in helping me on this project. Finally, to my exes. It wasn't always pretty, but may the pain we went through help many others.

CONTENTS

ACKNOWLEDGMENTS

A little over two years ago I started my blog: theproblemgays.com. The idea was to discuss LGBTQ+ issues in a voice I felt was missing from the landscape. I began covering what I felt was important to queer people: dating, relationships, legal issues, coming out, body image, sexual health, gay media, racism, depression, and more. My motivation was to be a source of information I did not have growing up. Coming out would have been much easier if I had someone relatable to guide me – I hoped to be that person to others.

Before my blog, I felt very disconnected from the LGBTQ+ community. Over time, I started having conversations with many of you who felt just as isolated. I spoke to many of you who found my views refreshing and, in turn, inspired me to expand and cover things with even more perspective. The Internet, of all places, connected me to the community in a way I had never experienced.

To anyone who has interacted with me online or found value in my content – thank you. Your encouragement is what inspired me to write this book and be so open. Ironically, I'm extremely private. My only motivation in memorializing these stories is that people may relate and hopefully gain insight from my past experiences.

The way our community connects and finds love has been turned upside down in the past decade. I hope that this book is a start to unraveling how we have been impacted.

[1] INTRODUCTION: JADED

I sat at a combination bakery and boba shop waiting for him to arrive. I was in a horrible mood, but here I was searching for love again. I was obsessed with finding a man, and I was looking for one who could instantly make up for all of my past dating failures. Every time a relationship failed, it seemed as though the stakes were higher. Who can I find that is better than the many disappointing dicks of my past? Who can I parade on social media, solidifying the caliber of man I can land to impress strangers on the Internet? When was I going to meet the man I finally deserved? The educated, successful, handsome, humble gentleman who wanted 2.5 kids – one in vitro, one adopted and the .5 a toss up – that would drive around with me in our blue metallic Volvo XC90 plug-in hybrid. The man I could finally introduce to my parents, who I have left grappling with the fact that they have a gay son for about five years but have never followed up by showing them proof of a boyfriend.

The years had jaded me. I tried to take breaks from dating apps but I had grown addicted to trying to erase my shitty dating history with some fictional new person who was going to be the answer to all of my problems. I started talking to this new guy a few days prior - let's call him Andrew. He quickly took a genuine interest in me. He was from the Midwest and had only been in LA for about a year. I wondered if the city had jaded him yet. Even if it had, it couldn't have been nearly as bad as the near decade of gay dating I had just been through.

I started my dating career hopeful, excited, nervous, and innocent. After having my heart crushed a couple of times, I don't think it ever recovered. I was meeting these guys without a heart at all. I wasn't necessarily emotionally unavailable, but I was the away message of emotion – might be back, but also, might leave this on so no one bothers me. These guys were meeting a body that looked pretty good and a mind that knew the right things to say.

Dating had become a conquest. Whether the men were good or bad didn't matter, because I had no heart or love to offer them. I just hoped that maybe if I got far enough with them, those things would magically come back. Not surprisingly, I didn't get very far with any of them.

I knew that this was an opportunity to meet a genuine guy after a slew of typically shallow LA dates, but I wasn't in the mood for it. I Facetimed Andrew the night prior and it went pretty well. We talked for hours and only stopped because we were falling asleep. Although I wasn't in the best mood for that Facetime, I still cracked enough jokes and conjured up the charm to sustain his interest.

Today was different. Today I was a bitch. Today I popped off at Andrew because we had a loose plan to hang out in the afternoon. I texted him the morning, and he didn't respond until 2 PM. He said he was at brunch with friends. 2 PM is that pivotal moment on a Sunday where you have to decide between doing something or sitting around until the new *Real Housewives*, falling asleep after, and dragging your ass into work the next day. So when I didn't hear from him until then, I decided to move on and make something of my day. He didn't realize I would be annoyed by the delay in his message and actually apologized profusely, but my mood was already fucked up. I was disappointed and over him. Once I get in that mood it is hard for me to snap out. I told him that, but he still wanted to meet and make it up to me.

Follow through in gay dating is extremely rare and sweet. I find myself meeting with guys that I otherwise feel will not be a good fit, simply because they show some basic effort. The guys that I think *are* a fit are the ones that make *me* do the chasing. That gets very old very fast. Effort is like the new "abs" of dating. Every morning text was one pack. Text me every morning for six days and you're suddenly the sexiest person I'm talking to.

Andrew seemed to know effort well. Or perhaps he was the first guy to be genuinely interested in me in a long time. Effort seems to come naturally when there is genuine interest. Regardless of the reason, here I was, at 4 PM on a Sunday about to meet him in an unfortunate mood. I was counting on him to turn it around but knew it would be very difficult for him to do so – especially on a first date where I should be putting in some effort too.

We locked eyes as I walked past the window and I came inside to hug him. He smiled. I didn't. He had such an authentic excitement and happiness in his face when he looked at me. Like, "Finally, this guy I've been vibing with for a few days is here! This is awesome." And here I came, thinking, "I can't believe you didn't text me until 2 because you were at brunch, you're lucky I showed up." We got in line and ordered some food. He paid – either out of guilt or because he was a gentleman. Probably because he was a gentleman - this guy was a class act. We sat down with our food and stared at each other. "So."

He was very perceptive, so I think he quickly realized that my mood was indeed not where it should be for a first date. We talked about the usual harmless topics, although we did know a fair bit about each other by this point. We struggled through a little more conversation about work, living situations, and things we enjoy doing. It was very generic conversation and I was admittedly giving him very little to work with.

It was almost like I was on the witness stand. My body is here; I'm answering your questions. I'm not being purposefully rude, but I'm not going out of my way to be nice either. I could be showing way more interest in you. It got cold and he went back to his car to get his jacket. "What the fuck is wrong with me?" I wondered. You finally have a good one in front of you. This genuine, unspoiled, Midwestern, former-Abercrombie-model-looking guy with a good job that wants to settle down and meet his life partner. Everything I had been seeking, give or take the Abercrombie. I sat there with my muffin and boba in the cold. I wonder if he would even come back, I didn't give him much reason to. He did come back a bit later. He sat down and said, "So." Not the same kind of "so" we started the conversation with. This was a "this isn't working" kind of "so." He said that I wasn't giving him much in the way of conversation, so it might be best for us to meet at a better time.

I felt bad because I knew he had driven an hour just to meet me here. We had been here for about 20 minutes. I clearly fucked it up. His beautiful blue eyes that were so excited to greet me had dulled. They were so profoundly sad and disappointed in me. I didn't know him well, but I had crushed him. Like a parasite, I infected him with my jadedness. I put a notch of disappointment into his gay dating belt. He would take this with him into his next date, trying a little less for the next guy. Guarding his heart more carefully. Not being as excited to meet someone urgently. Not putting much effort into first dates, just in case they went wrong. He would begin to screen guys for compatibility on Facetime, just like me. He would start putting gym time before dating, not texting guys back right away. The list goes on.

I told him I was sorry things went this way and he began to walk away. He asked me why I wasn't getting up. I said I wanted to sit there alone for a while. Me, my boba, my muffin, and my issues. A straight couple walked by. They were in love. Assholes. This was a tipping point for me. I knew I had become something of a monster - Grindr and app culture had ruined me over the years. I started innocent, happy, and eager, but one by one, these guys robbed me of something. I started full of charge and these men had me on low power mode. I was about to run out of battery.

I sat there reflecting on all of the Grindr interactions over the years: the bad coffee dates, the awkward sexual encounters, the catfish, the fights, the nudes, the thrill, the disappointment, the instant gratification. It had been 6 or 7 years of abuse now. Grindr was a drug, and I had used it recklessly. I extracted the rush I needed out of it and it slowly destroyed me. With no checks and no moderation, I had let it take over my life. Someone I could have potentially spent my life with walked away from me because I was holding a grudge over a text delay. I felt worthless and defeated. I needed to figure out how I got here. How could I stop this inadvertent cycle of gay men crushing gay men? What could I have done differently? The men of Grindr had slowly ruined me and I was on a quest to figure out how.

In this book, I dissect three of my early and impactful Grindr relationships in an attempt to unearth answers, extract lessons, and hopefully become a better person than I was for Andrew.

[2] LESSON ONE: CHRIS

You know those moments of desperation when you completely run out of guys to talk to? Maybe it's just me who depletes the supply that quickly. Well this was back in 2013 or so. I was in the full throes of needing constant male attention. I was single, gay, and working in Century City. For those who are fortunate enough not to be from LA, Century City is a corporate enclave between West LA and Beverly Hills where pretty entertainment and lawyer types eye fuck each other on their way to the Westfield food court for lunch. Since I couldn't successfully translate any of those eye fucks into a loving relationship, I found myself constantly refreshing Grindr, hoping that one of the men I just walked by would be recognizable enough to hit up. I think that was the motivation behind creating Grindr – letting you know if the cute guy near you is safely approachable. In reality, it was just a constant reminder that the cute guy near you is straight, gay and taken, or too classy to be bothered with dating on apps.

I was none of those things, so Grindr was my go-to for any hope in dating. In fact, I was getting so desperate that even regular Grindr was seemingly not enough. It was ultimately one of those Grindr Xtra free-for-seven-day promos that did me in. My grid of eligible gay men expanded from the normal 100 to 300. I was pulling in dick from the Valley at this point – the opportunities were endless.

Amidst my expanded sea of men, I found him…we'll call him Chris. My friends would always mention how he looked just like Chris Brown. I wish they could have warned me that he had just as many issues. He was 28, my age as I write this. At the time I was 23 and he seemed grown as fuck. If someone told me before I sent that first message that this guy would be taking me on the most passion-driven, tumultuous yearlong roller coaster of my early gay dating life, I would have thought twice.

I remember that even my first few messages with Chris were an argument. Is there a saying about the first interactions being an indication of the entire relationship? I remember what that early arguing was about, too. He was not being responsive enough to my messages. I am admittedly impatient on apps. When I finally find someone I like, I tend to wait around for their responses. I don't go crazy with it, but if I see that you were online two hours ago and didn't respond to my message from three hours ago, I get highly annoyed. Some may call that creepy or excessive; I call it romantic…with a touch of obsession.

Since Chris was continually unresponsive, I threatened to block him and move on. I used that tactic quite it bit because it is one of the few ways to take power back over your life when a guy isn't giving you the attention you need. "You know what? I'm done with you so this cannot impact me anymore." Perhaps that immaturity keeps me single to this day. Or perhaps I just know the attention I want and deserve.

This clearly enticed him. He seemed shocked at my drastic approach, but started talking to me a bit more. Perhaps my impatience was a combo red flag but also endearing. In gay dating, that is often considered a win because we typically just deal with red flags. Eventually we moved it to texting. I must have impressed him with my inordinate and detailed knowledge of amusing Tamar Braxton quotes.

Man, I'm tearing up as I write this because I just remembered how much I loved him. A pure love that is so hard for me to recapture these days. Fuck him. It could have been something. Spoiler alert.

<u>Meeting of the Minds</u>

A couple weeks after we first spoke, he pulled up to the Coffee Bean that would later be known as "our spot." I took a lot of my dates to this location, but Chris made such an impression on me that it will forever be known as "our spot." I guess to anyone reading this who later dates me; if we end up at a Coffee Bean, call me out on it.

I remember being impressed by his Infiniti SUV. As a car guy, the cars men choose to drive make an important impression on me. Not that they need to be fancy or anything, but it is a total statement on the type of person they are. For instance, a Prius driver is going to give me hell for my bougie tendencies, a BMW driver is going to be competitive with my bougie tendencies, and a Jeep driver is going to force me camping to reform my bougie tendencies.

It was telling that Chris' car was actually a rental, because most of my experience with Chris looked nicer on the outside than our reality. Before he even showed up we had another spirited text message exchange. He was at a brunch with his friends – from noon until around 7 PM. In fact, this is probably where my complex around gay men delaying me for brunch began. Chris and his friends seemed to be a close-knit and alcohol-dependent bunch of 30 somethings. I was shocked to learn that people considered that span of time appropriate for brunch. He was annoyed that I was calling him out on it. I finally convinced him to meet me, despite him not being sure about our connection. That was the undertone of the evening – uncertainty.

He was handsome. He had on a baseball hat and jeans that fit the right way. You know the way – not too tight, not too lose, allows me to see what you're working with but not so clearly that the gay barista can also see. He was my type of guy. We were probably there talking for two hours. The first hour was very tentative. He would throw out an idea, I would throw out an idea. We weren't sure of each other's sense of humor or interests. I am very opinionated and have a very dry sense of humor, so some of that was landing with him. I remember the first hour was exploratory, not really sure if it was going to work. The second hour was me making inroads - he was beginning to get hooked. There was a beautiful, human glow in his eye when I would say something surprising or funny. It was a banter-filled, flirtatious, argumentative conversation. When it was finally time to leave, I remember being sad that it was over. We hugged. He hugged hard – that probably ranks as one of the most satisfying gay feelings. To be hugged by a man that puts a strength and conviction into it that says, "I would be proud to have you." It's very different than a vanity, pat on the shoulder hug.

We finally got in our cars and left, him turning left in his Infiniti SUV and me turning right in my Audi SUV. Two difficult gay men insulated in the comfort of unnecessarily large and luxurious midsize sport utility vehicles. The whole drive home I knew this was going to be something. I got home and sent the text of truth. The "post-date if he responds immediately he had a good time and loves me" text. He responded.

Hindsight is 20/20, the cliché goes. There were so many early signs throughout my relationship with Chris that so vividly foreshadowed some of our eventual issues. In those first weeks after the Coffee Bean, we met for lunch during my break at a California Pizza Kitchen in Beverly Hills. I was at that stage of my career where it was not really acceptable to go to a sit-down lunch because I couldn't really be later than an hour. I risked it for him.

He met me there in a suit. I actually didn't like how he looked that day and reconsidered the whole thing. His hair was wrong – shallow much? Or maybe it was that once I parked my car and walked over to the CPK, I noticed him in his car. He honked aggressively at someone doing something trivial – taking too long to back out or something. I absolutely hate people who honk their horns because I think it's never that serious unless you're alerting someone of danger. He honked so fucking hard at such an unnecessary situation. I remember thinking, how could I ever date "the guy" that honks like that? I never told him I saw that.

It was no surprise that he and I had argued earlier in the day via text about something stupid. He knew he was wrong prior to coming to the lunch and drew me a cute "I'm sorry" note that he gave to me. I was impressed that he cared or noticed enough to acknowledge the issue. I never even understood whether he was mad at me or something that had happened at work. My recognition of Chris' "honking" attributes, counter-balanced with some of his romantic gestures, foreshadowed what would be an ongoing struggle in our relationship.

The Proposal

Despite some of these initial arguments and red flags, the early times were certainly good too. Probably one of the best days with Chris was the day we made things official. It was a day I planned from start to finish. I wonder if that had anything to do with its success? I didn't tell him anything. He met me at my house and we started driving. We went from Downtown LA to Malibu, one of my favorite secluded hikes. It took us a very long time to get there, with numerous back roads, and I could sense he was a bit nervous about how far we were getting from town. He questioned why we didn't hike at Runyon. Runyon is an extremely popular hiking trail near Hollywood, littered with people who want to be seen shirtless, walking their dogs with Starbucks in hand (no shade to the few people who genuinely hike and enjoy Runyon).

I told him I wanted to go on a real hike, one that felt like we were getting away from LA and seeing something different. The hike was a 10-mile journey – a test of our endurance for the mountain and each other. I had packed food and snacks for us and we even took my dog along. We had a lot of opportunities to talk and bond throughout the hike. Given the length of the hike, I'm sure he had many "where the fuck are we" moments through which he had to trust that I knew the path ahead. That was rare for him, so I appreciated the trust. Finally, around mile seven of the hike we came up to this beautiful overlook with a panoramic ocean view.

We had to climb through some overgrown shrubs to make it to the overlook. This is the part where the Runyon hikers would be scratching their abs with nature. It was a truly breathtaking spot. Ocean as far as the eye can see on an 85-degree Southern California day. I remember feeling extremely nervous. Fuck, do I want to do this? We already fight so much and it's only been several weeks. What if he takes it the wrong way?

I dug into the snack backpack and pulled out a ring box. I didn't know if I should get down on one knee or if he would make fun of me. I stayed standing. I knew I should have done the knee thing. He noticed the box and gave me that "what the actual fuck" look. I told him that I really liked him and how excited I was to be getting to know him over the past month. He kept looking at the box, extremely nervous. I opened the box and could hear my voice crack as I asked, "Chris, will you be my boyfriend?"

By now he was laughing in relief. The box had a watermelon Starburst in it. I learned that was his favorite flavor when he bought a whole bag at a gas station one day. I never knew anyone who actually bought Starbursts in adulthood besides grandmas.

For a few minutes there on top of the mountain we felt a new sensation of bliss in our relationship. He was so taken back at the shock of a dramatic candy proposal. I was so nervous that he was going to shut me down. It was such a pure moment of me putting my heart and feelings completely on the line for someone. He said yes.

I asked him if he thought it was too soon to be official. He reasoned that it wasn't, because no one had ever done anything like that for him. No one had planned a moment with that much effort and no one had the guts to put himself out there in that way. It didn't matter how soon the moment came, because he was impressed. Looking back, Chris was probably only beginning to like me at this moment, but I knew I loved him. Perhaps I didn't know what real love was – but it was the realest love I had ever felt for someone romantically. I was all in. I gave my heart to someone in like with me, and I was ok with it at the time.

As we drove home from the hike, Chris and I shared what would be another memorable moment in the car. I tend to be a person who sings while driving, but not typically with people I don't feel comfortable with. Although I was driving home with my newfound boyfriend, I still hardly felt comfortable with him. We barely knew anything substantial about one another at this point.

Browsing through songs, I jokingly bragged to him about my vocal ability. In actuality, I am semi-serious about my singing ability (see: elementary school honors choir years.) He dared me to sing something. I asked him to pick a song. One way or another, we landed on "Lost Without You" by Robin Thicke. For those unfamiliar, it is a highly romantic, slow-tempo, almost entirely falsetto love song. The verses are easy enough to get through, but dear Robin goes sky high in octave on the chorus. I made it through verse and chorus one, bringing down Robin's octave so I could maintain my vocal integrity. Do you like how I said I'm not serious about my singing and just said "vocal integrity?"

Well, Chris was not here for it. He said "it doesn't count if you bring it down an octave." I was struck with one of those "wow, you know what?" moments. On the next chorus, I struggled but successfully hit the full octave notes. It's one of those things you will lose your voice after, but I did it anyway. He didn't seem impressed or disappointed. I took his silence as a win.

Almost a year later, I would realize that he was secretly recording a video of me singing that song, explaining his silence. During one of our fights, he sent me that video after I accused him of not caring. I was blown away that in a moment where he seemed not to care, he was actually memorializing something that was special to him. Those little gestures made me love him in a way that transcended the petty fights and drama. He cared, but he just had a weird and secretive way of showing it.

In gay dating, we tend to run into a lot of that type of baggage. Maybe he was afraid to love, ashamed to show affection. Maybe he was afraid to be connected and depend on another man for happiness. Looking back now, we were both young. He seemed so mature at the time – but we were both just figuring things out.

I'm Coming Out

During one of those early Coffee Bean dates, we discussed an ever-pertinent question in gay dating. "How out are you?" At the time, I was in a transitory stage of my sexuality. I had experienced love once before, a yearlong relationship in which neither my boyfriend nor I were out. That break up was pretty difficult for me, so it felt like the right time afterward to come out to my friends about the relationship, as I needed their support. When you lose the one person you feel comfortable being yourself with, you are suddenly incentivized to be yourself with a lot more people.

So I told Chris that almost all of my friends knew about my sexuality, but I wasn't out to my family or at work. I quickly noticed that this was going to be an issue for him. At 28 years old, he was at a much more comfortable and open place with his sexuality and had fought a lot of the sexuality battles (internal and external) that I would soon be facing myself. He told me that it would be hard for him to date someone that wasn't out to his family. He made valid points. After all, how could you have a genuine and deep relationship with someone if you can't integrate into their family – generally a large portion of someone's life and heart? I wasn't ready to come out immediately to my family but I knew it was important to Chris.

Some months later I did ultimately come out to my family, something I never visualized happening so soon. I always thought it would be nice if I could be open with them, but was of course terrified of their reactions. They were ultimately supportive, as they knew I was going through a lot in life, including some major depression. Perhaps they felt that if I was open with my sexuality I could be happier overall. That was partially true, but not the full extent of my personal issues. I remember my mom being so open as to say that if I was dating anyone, I should bring them to Thanksgiving dinner. I think she had a perception that my secret former boyfriend (prior to Chris) was actually my current boyfriend, and that we were still together. She had met that boyfriend as a "friend" a couple times. I assured her that was not the situation.

It was Chris who I had in mind when the Thanksgiving dinner potential came up. That being said, I didn't feel that he and I were solid enough for any family introductions at that point. Part of me appreciates him for being that unwelcome, but perhaps necessary push I needed to come out to my family. Part of me wishes he didn't pressure me and offered an approach other than "rip off the Band-Aid." It's unfortunate that through all of our fighting and drama, he never got the benefit of integrating into that part of my life. I would never introduce my family to someone I wasn't completely solid and happy with, and we just never got that far. I did talk to him about my parents and their personalities, and he joked about how much they would like him as I would with stories of his parents. I bet they would have liked those positive aspects of him, and that he was making me happy. It's too bad.

One of the early mysteries in our relationship was the fact that Chris would not let me see where he lived. He said he lived in the valley, probably 25 minutes or so from my place downtown. He had come over to my place numerous times. I felt that I had a pretty nice place for my age. It was a studio apartment in a newer building with a cool view of the skyline from the balcony. I worked my ass off to get into a place like that, and was proud of the achievement. He would comment that "this place would be entirely too small for a couple." You know how some people find the one negative comment to make about something that is clearly good or nice? He was often that person. It's interesting, because young couples occupied most of the other studio apartments in that building.

His criticism made me quite curious about how he was living to so comfortably critique my situation. By the way, can you imagine not knowing where your literal boyfriend lives before classifying him as your boyfriend? I tried it. At any rate, I asked several times to see his place. I'm the type of person that only becomes more curious and aggressive when someone continuously avoids a topic. That's exactly what happened. He kept denying me the ability to come over, and I kept getting more upset about it. Looking back now, I can clearly see we had two very different and incompatible communication styles. The whole thing ultimately made me feel stupid. I wondered if I did the "boyfriend" thing too soon.

The only excuse he ever gave me was that his dad was staying with him so it would be uncomfortable for me to be there too. This always struck me as odd, since he also mentioned his dad was very well off and that they weren't particularly close. Wouldn't a rich dad you're not that close with just stay at a hotel? These excuses continued for quite some time and caused many fights between us.

The First Break-Up

One time, I recall that Chris fell off the map for a couple days and stopped responding to my texts, calls, and voicemails. Communication is everything to me in a relationship. I was firm in that, even at my young age. Even if I am mad at my partner, we need to communicate through our issues and work it out. So when Chris cut me off and disappeared, I got very angry and even depressed. I think when you really love someone, you place a lot of importance on them in your life. I'm still conflicted on how smart that is. Regardless, most of my happiness tends to emanate from my partner when I am in a relationship. Not hearing from a boyfriend for a couple days can flip those days upside down, completely messing up my mood at school, work, and even how I act with family and friends.

After two days of his silence, I had to take back my power from Chris. It was the only thing I had left. I texted him that our relationship was over and that it wasn't cool for him to disappear with no explanation. I couldn't take any more of being this upset and just needed to get back to me. I told him I had to start dating people who were more available. I made a new Grindr account that day and tried my best to move on.

A day or two later, I heard back from none other than Chris. This wasn't very welcome since I was trying to kill him in my mind so I could actually get off of the rollercoaster our short relationship had already become. I explained to him that I made a new Grindr and needed to find someone more compatible with me. He latched onto that. "Wow, you made another Grindr because I didn't talk to you for two days?" He accused me of cheating on him through this act, even though I told him "it was over" and hadn't even met up with anyone new at that point. For the rest of knowing him, he would twist this moment in his favor to brand me as a "cheater."

He loved this turn of events, because they gave him an edge. I was forever the bad guy after this. Mind you, on my end, he had disappeared from my life with no explanation and I had no idea if or when he was going to resume communication. Maybe he sensed what I was doing and came back knowing that he could turn the tables and make me feel bad. This is all because he – my supposed boyfriend – wouldn't let me go to his house. He was the one who didn't want to open up a part of his life to me, and now I had to pay for it. Me, the "cheater." I never figured out why he didn't invite me over. Maybe he didn't even have a place of his own. Maybe his dad was indeed over there. I would learn much later that Chris had a major problem with lying so I tend to believe that I never saw that place because it didn't exist.

Chris had a way of taking situations where he looked bad and flipping them against me. It was ironic that I was studying to be the lawyer and not him, because he would do great at manipulating circumstances before a jury. One night, at my place of course, we got into another fight. As I write about these continuous fights, years after they took place, I realize how deep I was in with this guy. The bad times clearly outweighed the good.

After this particular fight, I remember kicking him out of my apartment on a night he was planning to sleep over. I remember he really didn't want to leave. I kept trying to tell him how serious I was, and how he really needed to get out of my space. It was probably 2 AM. He threw around some threats like how he would never talk to me again if I indeed kicked him out. That silence would be music to my ears at that point. He finally left. We didn't talk for several days, but somehow we resumed conversation after the blowout.

This tended to happen, and I had a habit of missing him immensely because I actually loved him and depended on his communication in my daily life. I would always think of the right words and apology to get him back. If you looked at our text logs after a fight, it would be huge paragraph blocks of messages from me before he gave in. I think he would fall for the amount of effort I was putting into getting him back and knew I cared. I don't think he loved me the way I loved him, though. Or he didn't show it, if so. He always had a wall up with me ever since that couple day break up and remaking of Grindr incident.

My romantic ideal of missing him was swiftly met with one of Chris' sobering reality checks. On this occasion, after I kicked him out at 2 AM, he claimed that a homeless man robbed him outside of my building at gunpoint. I lived downtown and there were a lot of sketchy characters, so I had to believe him and felt absolutely horrible. If I hadn't kicked him out at 2 AM, this wouldn't have happened to him. I wondered why he didn't just walk to his car right after walking out of my building? He claimed he was outside standing around crying about our fight, when the man came up to him and caught him off guard. On a subsequent hang out, I noticed that he had a different wallet than he usually did. He claimed that it was a back up wallet, since he lost his original wallet in the gunpoint incident. Whether he was lying or not, he seemed to put enough detail into the stories to make them quite believable.

Later on in our relationship, I would uncover lies that eventually led me to question everything he told me, including the gunpoint story. Nonetheless, I felt horrible for quite some time after this. Once again, he turned me kicking him out into a complete sob story for himself. Whether it happened or not, the manipulation in our relationship was persistent enough that I had to wonder if that was a lie, too.

The Gift Wars

One of the "good" aspects of my relationship with Chris early on turned out to be ultimately problematic. Chris was very into gift giving and planning dates. It was a refreshing and sweet gesture – one that I had little experience with in gay dating. I remember one time he came over, just on a regular day, with a bunch of wrapped gifts. I was shocked that someone would think to be so kind on a day that wasn't a birthday or holiday.

Your early 20's are a time in life when "gift" excitement is usually over. By that point in life, I was more excited to give gifts than receive them, probably because I wanted unattainable things like a Porsche rather than a Nintendo 64. But here was Chris with gifts for me – and I was excited. They were not only things I wanted, but also things with meaning behind them. Nothing over the top in extravagance, but they weren't cheap either. I remember one gift was a pair of Jordan's. I had always joked with him about how I wanted a pair but was too intimidated to buy or wear them and be branded a poser. I remember he bought me a GoPro camera to mount to my motorcycle helmet. I had recently purchased my dream bike to ride to work and school, but barely knew what I was doing. I guess the GoPro was the gift of evidence if I ever got into an accident. He also mentioned I could try to make cool riding videos with it. Whenever he brought me gifts he always included some for my dog. Talk about the way to my heart - to think about my dog *and* me. It was always so cute and impressive.

He also liked to plan dates. He didn't seem to like sitting around, ever. Of course, being older, he was in a different financial place than I was. He could afford to go out to more fancy dinners, concerts, and experiences. I felt a little out of my league at times but he never seemed to bring up that financial disparity. It was probably unnoticeable to him since I was quite the little spender those days (of my limited funds).

Where the gift giving and date planning went wrong was that it created expectations. It seems like we were always trying to one-up each other with gifts or by planning the more impressive date. I'll admit that it was exhilarating and fun for a while. Trying to be romantic at a level beyond my years. Honestly, maybe I started this all with my boyfriend "proposal," a true experience from start to finish. The thing about that experience is that it didn't cost much money. It was about being thoughtful and impressive, but not necessarily extravagant.

I wouldn't say he relied on money to impress me, but he probably had less time to plan experiences so it was easier and more familiar for him to make reservations or buy tickets. Personally, I did not like to go out very much. So all of his nights on the town became a point of contention for me. It was something I did for him, but didn't necessarily enjoy. It was something I did to feel like an "adult." I did it to feel like a vital gay man dating in his late 20's, when I was really just figuring out who I was in my early 20's.

Whenever I would complain about going out, he would throw in my face that I was ungrateful about the effort he was putting into the relationship. I would explain to him that effort, to me, is not making a reservation or going to the coolest new spot in LA. Effort, to me, could happen chilling at home. I wanted to spend time and bond with him, which is not particularly easy to do in a noisy restaurant. It was clear that we were on opposite ends of the going out spectrum.

The same thing would happen with the gifts. I would find myself buying things that I didn't necessarily have the money for, just to keep up with him. It seemed like he didn't ever appreciate them as much as I appreciated his. Looking back now, it was a clear-cut competition between us. When he felt like I was winning, he became jealous and unhappy. When I felt like he was winning, I felt inadequate and one-upped. We were both losers in this game.

Fan-Fucking-Tastic

A time that I felt completely shut down by Chris was around our first Valentine's Day together. In the weeks preceding, I was in his car and noticed he was listening to Fantasia's latest album. I didn't really peg him for a Fantasia fan, and I personally didn't love nor hate Fantasia. Perhaps I didn't know enough of her music at the time (that is, until *Drag Race* featured "Even Angels" on a lip-synch for your life and she became – no lie- one of my iTunes top played songs of all time). I thought it was kind of cute that he was listening to Fantasia and he made a comment, perhaps in jest, that he "loved his girl Fantasia." Based upon that knowledge, for Valentine's Day, I bought us tickets to the Fantasia concert in Chicago. I hated traveling, and I was terrified of flying. I hadn't flown in quite some years so I thought this would be a pivotal trip for us.

First, I thought I was being thoughtful by getting us Fantasia tickets since he seemed to like her and I was open to hearing more of her music. More importantly, it would be our first trip to a distant city together, a true test of how we got along. Finally, I was going to be depending on him to comfort me through my first flight in a very long time. He knew I was anti-flying, and I was still afraid to do it, but for him I was going to.

I remember agonizing over which seats to get on Ticketmaster. Every tier of seats getting more and more expensive, but not wanting him to comment on how far we were from the stage. Looking back, what an asshole he was for making me internalize his expectations and giving me anxiety over spending money on him. Nonetheless, I pulled the trigger and bought expensive tickets.

I gave them to him to open and he didn't really react. You know when you don't get that instant "wow" reaction to a gift so you start explaining it, trying to help the person understand how amazing it is? So, I started. "Well, I know you like her music and I thought it would be cool for us to go on a weekend trip. It would be my first flight and I'm nervous but you'll be with me." He responded that he didn't actually like Fantasia that much. He was just joking when he said he did. And "why would we go to Chicago? Do you know how cold it is this time of year?" The whole thing went over his head. He made me feel like shit over what was supposed to be a special moment, so I withdrew and stopped talking. He tried to ask what was wrong but I didn't respond – even an asshole like him should know what went wrong. Days later, I remember calling up Ticketmaster to get a refund on my tickets. I remember the sassy rep on the phone said "you're cancelling on your girl Fantasia?!" I couldn't help but chuckle.

I never fully understood what Chris did for work. He was supposedly in finance but despite all of my Googling and reverse-image searching (thank you Catfish for starting around this time), I could never pull him up. I would spend hours trying to find a receipt on this guy. I knew he had to do something; after all, he had recently purchased a new BMW and seemed to have all this money for gifts and going out. He seemed to complain about work a lot, and said he had an assistant. He spoke in significant detail about his days and trips he would have to take for work and projects that were happening. He would mention things his coworkers did that annoyed him. Thinking back, I do think he did more or less what he said he did, but aspects of it were probably exaggerated.

When I would tell my friends about him they would definitely raise an eyebrow or two. Around New Year's, he had apparently received a major promotion because his boss was leaving the company. He said that he was taking a bunch of classes to get the necessary clearances to basically take over his boss' job. I remember on New Year's Eve he had to go to a work party and was going to stop by my place afterward. I'm not sure if it was ever a thought for me to go to the New Year's party with him, or if we were too fresh at that point. At any rate, he turned up at my place later that night in a weird mood. He was upset that I didn't want to go out, but at that point it was pretty late in the evening. He also knew that I generally didn't like going out, so a last minute New Year's run was not my idea of fun.

I think it was still before midnight – maybe 11 PM or so. I wanted to stay in and have a quiet and reflective New Year's together. I remember us having an argument that tainted the New Year's kiss, and then basically trying to make up afterward to salvage the night. He wanted to have sex and I didn't really feel like it. He, of course, threw in my face that it was a special night and I was ruining it. Some say the way you spend your New Year's dictates the mood for the rest of the year. The fact that I had eye-rolling, uncomfortable intimacy with someone I constantly fought with was a dead-on mood for 2014.

Through our many highs and lows, our volatile relationship struggled on. Together, not together, apologizing, back together. It was a seemingly endless cycle. Some of these "off" periods would last for quite a while. It was usually me calling things off in frustration and trying to stay as strong as possible, not returning to the cycle…but the naïve romantic in me would always go back.

Chris would never make it easy to go back either. I'd text and email endlessly, I'd leave voicemails. They would contain long and elaborate apologies and signs as to why we belong together. I would explain things I had learned since the last break up and why I thought I could make it better. It always seemed to be me who was begging him to take me back. I guess I always knew that there was something intrinsically wrong with that arrangement. If this guy actually loved me and was worth my time, shouldn't he ever be making the move? Like any other situation involving some manipulation and emotional abuse, the victim seemed to take the blame. I knew it was wrong, but the concept of love, the romantic ideal of "the one" pushes you to abort logic and make stupid decisions. I had never fought so hard for someone who could literally care less about me.

A Fresh Start?

One of the early nails in what was ultimately a titanium coffin was when Chris moved about 30 miles away from the city. He claimed that he wanted to start fresh and simplify his life away from LA. We were not together at this time. Shortly after expressing his desire to move, we actually stopped speaking altogether.

I knew where he had generally moved to, but had never been invited. I was cutoff from him and I became fixated on how to get him back, yet again. So, in a line of reasoning that made absolutely no sense, I decided that I also wanted to move to the area he moved to. I convinced myself of numerous reasons why I was interested in the move, because I was clearly aware of how crazy it was going to look. I too, decided, I wanted something different. Rent was cheaper in the area; it was close to the beach and could provide a different lifestyle. My lease ended and sure enough, I moved approximately two blocks away from Chris, my ex-boyfriend that was not speaking to me. Despite all of my half-baked reasons about why the move would be good for me, it was ultimately problematic. Some days, the traffic made my commute to work almost two hours long. It was equally far from my school, which I attended at night. It was basically miserable and inconvenient, but the romantic in me had a plan.

The romantic in me made a Grindr account and tried to find my ex-boyfriend online. I was blocked from his number at the time so this was my only option. Night after night, I would hop on Grindr and try to locate him. Was he one of the gray accounts with no profile picture? Was he this guy that was completely cropped? Did he change his age or details so he couldn't be tracked? It was about the second week after I moved in when I finally found him. My profile included my picture so he would immediately know it was me.

He was actually using the same profile picture from over a year ago when I originally met him. Way to rebrand yourself buddy! "Hi Chris," I messaged; completely ready for the colossal, nearly vertical fall this roller coaster was about to take me on. He was shocked to say the least. "What are you doing down here?" he nervously asked. I told him that I moved here. He laughed, reasoning that I might have been down there for dinner or to see friends. We went back and forth on this for ten minutes before he actually believed that I moved two blocks away from him. "Why the hell would you do that?" was his logical next question. "To be closer to you," I explained. Another ten minutes followed where he was shocked and upset, still in disbelief that anyone would sign a lease to move near an ex that wasn't even speaking to them. A two year lease, at that. I felt stupid and crazy during this conversation, but I knew from the beginning it would be a tough concept to approach Chris with. I was comforted that he was at least speaking to me and that, with time, I could turn it around as I had done many times before.

Our conversation probably started at 11 PM, and it was close to 4 AM before it ended. We talked about everything. He was pretty mad that I was ruining his "fresh start" by moving so close to him. We talked a lot about my reasons, and whether or not I actually did this for him. We talked about why I thought it was cool to secretly do all of this and then track him down on Grindr of all places. We discussed the fact that our relationship had been on and off probably ten times at this point. He kept saying that this was a waste of our time and that I was psychotic. I kept telling him that I loved him, and I felt that one reason why things didn't work out was that we didn't live close to one another. The distance made it stressful to plan things and being closer, we could finally have a carefree relationship. We could give it a fresh start. We could explore a new area together and hang out all the time.

It seemed that I was trying to force a perfect relationship on us.

I was trying to stuff a Ken doll into my Barbie Corvette that had too much baggage in the passenger seat to accommodate him. It just wasn't going to work. Both of us were always working plus I had school, how was living closer going to help when we both got home at midnight? I remember sending him videos during this conversation. They were recorded proclamations of my love and how serious I was about this. It was an exhausting night, but it didn't end with a "hell no" from Chris. I had some hope. My plan was coming together. We were going to fall in love and be together whether he liked it or not. I had invested so much time and emotion into this damn man. I felt that he owed me his love. It was pretty sick and twisted, but it felt like my only option. In retrospect, I can see how close I was to emotional rock bottom.

I eventually started to convince him to hang out with me around town. It started on the weekends when I figured he'd be home. We'd try a local restaurant. The love was very tenuous, to say the least. It constantly felt like I was three comments away from starting a fight at every dinner. The vibe was that he really didn't want to be there, but I think a small part of him did buy into the fact that we might be able to make things work since we lived closer. I was on my best behavior during these touchy times. In a lot of ways, I felt like I was tiptoeing on the edge of a volcano. This man was ready to blow at any moment and it was always me in the position to need to prove to him why this was a good idea.

I had to prove how I could change myself to make our relationship better, despite knowing that he was the majority of the problem. Although uncomfortable with the fragility of our new relationship, aspects of it made me very happy. I could just call up my man and walk over to his house. We could lounge around. We could sleepover. It appeared like what I thought a relationship should be. It's sad how I was just seeking the many simple assurances of a relationship that others take for granted. Eating together, running errands together, walking together, talking together. That's all I really wanted. Although I was getting a small taste of these things, it felt like a full time job to keep Chris happy and into me. It's clear to me now how uneven our relationship was.

One of the most upsetting moments in our relationship came out of a casual day at his place. We had gotten take out from California Pizza Kitchen. I realize this story will make it two tumultuous CPK incidents in our relationship – I wish I could say the pizza was the root of our issues, and not Chris' pettiness. We were watching something like *Basketball Wives*. What could go wrong?

Around this time, I had mentioned to Chris that I wanted to "have abs." I felt like I was putting on a few extra pounds and that I wanted to work out more. Perhaps the years of scrolling through seemingly perfect men on the grids of apps made me feel unworthy. I know many young gay men relate – we all wonder if those hot guys that never respond to us would actually notice if we had a bicep or embraced leg day. Some of us feel like our bodies are holding us back from interacting with the Grindr elite.

After years in the gay dating game, I can assure you that the Grindr elite are just a bunch of douchebags with nice bodies and no self-esteem. They will ignore you on dates so they can update their social media. They have nothing interesting to say and they will make you question your own sanity and self esteem. With that knowledge, I hope you can now eat the donut you're eyeing and stop caring. Working out should be for you and your health, not to impress others.

But at this point in time, I wanted abs. The thing is, I was still below the average weight for my height. The reason I note that detail is to underline what happens next. The moment I started eating the bread in my meal, Chris snatched it out of my hand. I was extremely upset. "What the fuck are you doing?" I yelled. He said that I needed to stop eating if I wanted to lose the weight. Now…I was raised never to mess with anyone's food. I believe that it is extremely disrespectful to take the food out of someone's hand as they are biting into it. It's not like I was a drug addict shooting up heroine and he was grabbing the needle from me. I was a relatively thin boy eating my bread and he snatched it. Not only that – he threw it away. We had a blowout argument over this. I explained how completely uncool it was to do what he did. He said it wasn't that big of a deal. I was beginning to see how controlling Chris was.

I reflected on some of the other times he would "shh" me during dinners. Ladies – if a man constantly tries to silence you, that's *his* insecurity with who you are and the things you're saying. Total red flag! It's like he was always trying to control me, and if it didn't go his way, he would ruin our time together. If you had any type of opinion about anything, it would turn into a fight. He kicked me out of his apartment that day and I was crushed. How did this seemingly perfect couples day turn into this type of fight? How badly had this guy been hurt in the past for him to think this behavior and accompanying level of anger was normal?

I knew a bit about Chris' past. Slowly he had revealed that he had suffered some abuse in his childhood. He had mentioned that he used to be overweight and lost a bunch of weight years ago. I always had these issues running in the back of my mind. Perhaps this is why I gave him so many chances. In a way, it was admirable that he was opening up to me and clearly I had no issue working through and overcoming challenges. What I didn't realize at the time is there is a difference between working through challenges together and simply taking someone else's abuse. Letting them lash out at you without a conversation or steps to reconcile. I kept wanting to fix Chris. We were going to work through his issues, our issues – we were going to fix it all and exist happily. A part of me was attracted to the challenge.

In gay dating, I had come across many types of men. There were many who were undoubtedly nicer and more into me than Chris, but he had a unique set of characteristics that made me want to fight for him. His demeanor, periodic thoughtfulness, intelligence, style, success, and not to mention our mutual interest in trash reality TV. On paper, he was whom I wanted to be with. He was the one I wanted to show off. It was worth the drama because in the end, nothing good comes easily. Or was it that love should be effortless? I would never fully know which dating philosophy was correct. Was I attracted to the challenge, attracted to him, or attracted to him but only on paper? It was confusing to say the least.

We of course overcame "bread-gate" because he manipulated the facts to make me believe that I overreacted and he was rightfully trying to help me reach my abdominal goals – and I bought it. Abuse 101. I continued on my endless quest to have cute dates and moments with Chris. After all, I didn't move near him just to suffer the daily traffic misery and general life inconvenience. It's funny; some people take law school so seriously. They live across the street from campus and take out loans so they don't have to work. They do anything they can to make sure they are focused on studying. What was I doing? Working full time, living two hours away from campus, chasing a guy who didn't want me, and still managing to do pretty well in class despite lacking the energy provided by carbs I was now not allowed to eat in Chris' presence.

It was right around this time that I became intent on us going to the OC Fair, an annual event in Orange County with fair foods, performances, and rides. It would be a really cute date – the type of place they would go to on 7th Heaven. I wanted it and deserved it. Chris seemed to be into the idea, which was rare when I was planning something. I remember we drove all the way to the OC Fair gate. The gate said that the fair was closed. We Googled it and sure enough, it wasn't even open that week. Chris was defeated, but I was not going to waste the rare and mutually good intentions of the day. We headed to Dave and Buster's and had a similarly fun and innocent time. This was one of the days that gratified me in my decision to move near Chris.

We were having some, albeit few, happy moments. Happier moments than we had experienced in a long time. I remember driving back home from Dave and Buster's, one hand on the steering wheel and one hand holding his. He was mine again. He was a headache, but a cute and successful headache and he was mine. It would be much later when he told me that my gesture of holding his hand on that drive warmed his heart. It was a moment that solidified to him that I was invested in him and not going anywhere. Things were finally looking up.

<u>Vegas Turn Up and U-Turn</u>

I had been waiting to exhale for probably six months at this point. We were back together, we were relatively happy. We could make this thing work. It was time for our next big relationship hurdle. We had known each other for over a year with the on-and-off title of "boyfriend," never having met each other's friends. The opportunity arose when Chris was invited to his friend's birthday party in Las Vegas. I love Las Vegas, and knew this would be the perfect opportunity for us to conquer a couple's trip and also "meet the friends." I figured they probably knew about me at this point unless he was weird and kept me a secret. I could usually get anyone to like me, so I knew I could impress his friends and they would solidify to him that I was a keeper.

I don't think Chris really wanted me to go on this trip with him. His friends were sacred to him, and I think deep down he feared that they would like me, negating his own leverage in continuing to hate me. Totally romantic, healthy relationship stuff! Aren't all relationships an endless power struggle for leverage during arguments? One way or another, I convinced him to take me to Vegas. I drove. I didn't realize I was navigating the descent into my personal hell, the flames for which were doused by Grey Goose vodka.

The drive to Vegas was relatively enjoyable. One thing that we always seemed to agree on was music. Rihanna was the glue that held us together. I wonder how many other gay people have said that before. At any rate, we pulled into a hotel I can't even remember. Planet Hollywood, perhaps. It was not a place I had ever stayed before. He mentioned one of his girlfriends was at the bar, drinking alone. I thought this was an odd thing to be doing in Vegas, but we parked the car and with our luggage, met up with "girl at bar" friend first. Since Chris was in his late 20's, most of his friends were in their 30's. This was a little different for me, being the early-20-year-old dating the "older man." I wasn't deterred by age, however. After all, I was mature enough for Chris so I would probably be mature enough for his friends. By the end of this trip, I realized I was actually more mature than all of them.

You know those 30-somethings that still hit the Vegas clubs as hard as the 21-year-olds? That was my weekend in a nutshell. I mentioned I love Vegas. The reason I love it is for the pools, the restaurants, the heat, and the general dystopian desert aesthetic. The clubs were a place I was forced to in my younger years and never, ever planned on returning. I remembered feeling awkward at the bar. I was introduced to his friend but he was mostly catching up with her and not including me too much. I just kind of sat near them, with my luggage, nodding sometimes and wishing I were one of the grandmas on the slots.

Chris finally had to go to the bathroom and I welcomed the reprieve. I started chopping it up with his friend and realized she was your typical, happy-to-be-in-Vegas-Drake-loving-down-ass-chick. I remember bonding with her over his latest album, about how men suck, and cracking the jokes necessary to get her on my side. Chris came back, of course curious if we had spoken about him. She said something like "I love this guy Chris! Good job with this one." He was visibly annoyed that I had impressed friend one. "Keep 'em coming," I thought – this weekend would be a breeze.

We arrived on Saturday, the big turn up night, and were going home the next day. Time was limited to cram in the fun. I remember trying my best to be a trooper the whole weekend. Not being a big drinker or clubber, I knew that was what these people – my elders – wanted to do. I remember getting ready with Chris in the hotel room and feeling like a "real couple." Do you ever have those moments? Where you perpetually feel 12 years old and it's super weird to be doing grown folks things? That's how I felt, but it still felt good. It felt like a reward for the hard work I was putting into this guy. Things were going so well that I just wanted to stay in the room with him for the night, but no such luck. Within hours of arriving, I found myself in a large suite at the hotel, pre-gaming with ten of his closest friends.

The birthday was for a straight man. I think he mistook pre-gaming for getting wasted, but that was none of my business. I remember talking to a few more of Chris' friends – even the straight guys – and making inroads. Many of you can relate to how uncomfortable it can be to talk to straight men at a party. It usually requires me to fake an understanding of beer or whatever sport is on that day. It became clear that Chris didn't really bring boyfriends or guys he was dating around too often. The weird part was that one of the guys didn't even know Chris was gay. I believe he thought I was a friend until someone explained it to him. After that, he was drunkenly overjoyed that Chris was gay and had a boyfriend. I remember being surprised that supposedly "close friends" didn't even know about his sexuality. Ironic, since Chris put so much pressure on me to come out. But I let it slide. Drake was blasted on Bluetooth speakers and shots of Grey Goose were consumed. Not being a drinker, I am even less so a shot guy. I remembered taking multiple to play along. Chris seemed ok at this point, mostly distracted with catching up with friends. He would leave me alone from time to time and I socialized just fine. Shortly after, we found ourselves in the nightclub at Bellagio.

You know that feeling when your soul removes itself from your body and you're kind of looking down on everything like "how the fuck did I get here?" That was the nightclub experience in a nutshell. People who were too damn old to be doing this (in my now-their-age-as-I-write-this opinion) were drunk, dancing, fighting, and screaming around me. I was buzzed, but not enough to forget the fact that I hated being there. I played along, doing everything Chris did. I also became aware that this was going to be one of our first "gay couple dancing at a club" experiences. A straight club, nonetheless. I was nervous of being judged by his friends and also Las Vegas. I'm not sure why, since none of them would remember this experience tomorrow. We fumbled through some dancing, and it was less awkward since we were in a group with women. Those moments are sometimes comforting but sad to me. The fact that two men dancing together would probably have sparked some sort of gay-bashing in this same setting.

Nonetheless, I continued to drink, I danced, and ultimately I proved that I can "hang" with his people. I'm not sure if he was impressed or not, but I was happy with the fact that at least he wasn't upset. At one point, he became annoyed with one of his friends and we abruptly left the club. There's nothing like the transition from the euphoria of a Vegas club to the humid garbage that is the Vegas Strip after midnight. We were pretty dressed up and I guess we gave off "gay couple" vibes to the extent that some passerby made a gay or fag remark toward us. Typical Vegas.

Now, in addition to teaching me not to grab bread out of people's hands, my parents taught me to be non-confrontational – especially in Vegas. It's really not worth fighting with a drunken idiot on the Strip, as things can easily escalate. Chris, with his alternative upbringing, started exchanging words with the guy. I got nervous and angry with him for engaging. He said that you "have to" engage with these people so they know you're not intimidated by them. I think a lot of guys in prison on felony assault charges share that philosophy. The dichotomy between Chris and I had never been so apparent. What the fuck was I doing in Vegas with this guy?

We eventually made it back into the relative safety of our hotel. Unrelated, my grandmother had recently passed away and it was something I was recalling at the time. She loved Vegas and this was the first time I had returned since her passing. I had fond memories of her playing slots on probably one the last trips before she was sent to a convalescent home. I told Chris I wanted to play slots in her memory. This, of course, didn't turn into a bonding moment for us.

He said something like it was inconvenient to do that right now, I got mad, and he said "fine lets do it." I was over the moment, and we ended up back in our room on unpleasant terms. Here we were, negative as fuck in the hotel room that we had left rather happily hours ago. This was my big "adult" Vegas hotel room alone with my boyfriend moment, except it was entirely fucked up. I think he took a shower at this point and I hoped that he emerged in a better mood. He didn't. I remember trying to cuddle to feel some sort of connection in the silent room. It didn't work, but eventually he started talking.

"I know about you," he said. I audibly rolled my eyes and asked what the hell he was talking about. He said "I know everything, everything you're hiding." Since I was literally hiding nothing from him, my agitation reawakened and I continued to ask what the hell he was talking about. "It's a small world," he said, "the guy at work you're hooking up with – I know all about it." I was at a complete loss for what was going on. I worked at a law firm with about 50 people; I wasn't even out at work and the only gay guy I could think of was about 45 years old and the opposite of my type.

I told him all of this and why none of what he was saying made sense. He didn't buy it – he continued with his revelations. How he knew someone from my past and how that person had told him "everything." Since I only had one committed relationship before, I still had no idea who he was talking about. I was single at all other times in my life prior to meeting him so what could I have done wrong? I began thinking and thinking – what was this sin he had on me? I remember a lot of yelling this evening. You're dealing with a really sick individual when they can just make up a lie to see how you will react to it. I think his twisted strategy was to come up with a relatively plausible story (hooking up with the work guy), and getting me to admit to some other transgression. In this case, his "plausible story" made no sense in the context of my workplace and the whole thing blew up in his face. I debated getting in my car and driving home alone, but it was 2 or 3 in the morning and even I was too tired to pull that off. We slept under a cloud of new cheating accusations. This guy would never trust me. Ever since that very first incident where he ignored me, I broke up with him, and made a Grindr account. I realized that the trust he lost in me at that time was never regained. This was never going to work.

The next morning we started the drive back home. It was relatively silent, but we did exchange some words. I'm not sure if the prior night's antics were alcohol driven but I was sober enough to be very upset with him. We didn't talk about the fight. I wanted to make it back home in relative peace. What a trip. I jumped through hurdles and went completely out of my comfort zone to get his friends to like me. His friends loved me and in fact, Chris was the one who ultimately got annoyed with his own friends. It seems that he later retaliated against me by making up a lie to try to catch me cheating. My only guess is that his goal was to justify why I wasn't as great as his friends thought I was.

We were halfway home when he asked if he could play music from his phone instead of mine. The new Beyoncé album had come out. He played "Drunk in Love." Like the rest of gay America, the song blew me away. Maybe it's just me, but don't we all remember where we were in the world when we heard a new Beyoncé album? I thought it was such a shame that I wasted this fresh Bey moment on a Vegas drive home with a lying manipulator that was mad his friends loved me more than he did. He was probably still drunk. I was no longer in love.

I needed a break from Chris. Perhaps he felt some guilt about what he tried to pull in Vegas, which he still had not produced evidence on. He never apologized, but I knew that I did nothing wrong and therefore felt no guilt. In the weeks following, we managed to continue going on dates in the "we live so close" mindset. I know that if he actually believed his accusations to be true, he wouldn't be hanging out with me at all. I'm not sure why I wasn't done with him at this point other than the fact that I had invested so much time and effort into the situation. For the first time in the year and a half, I was the one who remained unsure about our future. I guess I was waiting for him to make it up to me. From his end, he was probably "tolerating" me and overlooking my alleged cheating with my coworker.

Up All Night

Around this time, my friend had gotten free tickets to the One Direction concert through work. I guess now is the part of the book where I admit that I had a One Direction, and particularly, a Zayn obsession throughout this period. I was excited to get as close to Zayn as thousands of other tween girls would allow. Chris, not having met my friends or given me any consistency of peace or happiness in our relationship, was not invited. With this free time, he conspired to create what was ultimately the worst night of my relationship with him. Yes- after all of this, the worst night had yet to come.

"That's what makes you beau-ti-ful!!" the band shouted at the Rose Bowl, while lackadaisically jumping around. It always astonished me how One Direction didn't even need to dance like the *NSYNC's of my own time. They got paid millions for singing vocally unchallenging songs and bopping around stage. I guess the sad part was that we were all thoroughly entertained and enjoying the show.

After shedding an emotional tear of joy during "You and I," the night took a turn for the worse. I noticed my phone kept lighting up with text messages from Chris. I thought maybe he was checking in to see if I was having a good time. It was a weeknight, so I figured he was home from work by now watching *Love and Hip Hop* or something. That was one aspect of him I really liked – he watched the same trash as me. I finally checked the messages. "I can't believe you would do this." "You really must be having fun doing this shit." "I can't believe I ever let you back into my life." I rolled my eyes while my friends were singing along to the next song. What the fuck was this guy up to this time? I asked him what he was talking about. He said he knew what I was doing at the concert. I said, yes, enjoying One Direction. He thought otherwise. He said he claimed to know that I was on Grindr during the concert cheating on him. And so began my night from hell.

The last time I had a Grindr account was when I moved to be near him and was using the app to find him and implore that he take me back. Would someone that desperate for another's love spoil it by cruising on Grindr at a One Direction concert on a Thursday night with four girlfriends and a sea of tween girls? Who was I cruising for exactly, one of their dads in the parking lot? History showed that logic never coincided with Chris' cheating allegations. I assured him that I was not on Grindr and had never been since we were trying to make things work again.

My next thought was how he even would be able to confirm such a fact, unless he was driving around outside of the Rose Bowl specifically trying to catch me? Or was he making up lies to get me to admit something again? This was before Grindr had any searching functionality for locations other than where you currently were. God, is this the new way of gays aging themselves? "I remember the old Grindr, where you actually had to put effort into cruising." I digress. Chris stated that he would never be stalking me in that way. I didn't believe him.

His alibi was that his teenage cousin was also at the One Direction concert that evening. Since he was suspicious that I had been cheating on him since Vegas, he claims that he had his *female* teenage cousin (who I had never met and who probably didn't even know about me) make a Grindr account just to check if I was online at the concert. This was a twisted stretch of an alibi. Who would subject an innocent teenage girl to the Grindr grid on a manhunt for a man she has never met and who you seem not to even like all that much? Chris was also notoriously private, so I doubt he would spill tea with his teenage cousin on our shitty back and forth relationship and the many ways he felt I had wronged him.

Nonetheless, Chris adamantly continued with the allegations. The concert was over and we were making our way back on the trek to the parking lot. I remember we had parked in some VIP section up front that worked against us, because we ended up being the last cars to leave the parking lot. This is notable because I was in a text war with Chris for basically two hours after the concert had ended. My friend kept asking what was going on, as I was completely engrossed in my phone. I calmly said just some bullshit with Chris, again. Unlike Chris, I shared quite a bit with my friends about the ups and downs of our relationship. Needless to say, none of them were shocked that Chris was giving me drama at this point.

I explained his Grindr allegations and they obviously knew none of that was going on – knowing my character and also being right next to me the entire concert as I screamed my lungs out like a middle school girl. The implausibility of his allegations was actually pretty funny to them. That's how stupid it was. I knew, however, that the night was far from over for me. After dropping my friends off, I started my drive home. It was always an extra thirty minutes away. Thirty of those minutes were always spent contemplating why I would move this far to live near someone making me this miserable. I had come to a ceasefire in the text war and asked Chris if I could just stop by his apartment on my way home to figure this all out. He begrudgingly agreed.

The next hour of my life was very *The Hills*. For those of you who haven't watched the show, what I mean is that the drama that ensued was so theatrical that it would make MTV cameras envious. I pulled up to his luxury waterside apartment complex in my BMW M3. He always thought I copied him by buying that car, as he constantly reminded me how he had the same exact car years before me. He was standing outside as my curve-illuminating bi-xenon headlights highlighted the jogger sweats he wore that would make me melt. "This asshole wants to look cute for this," I remember thinking. I also remember wishing that cameras *were* there – because the venom I had within me was about to make amazing TV.

When I moved to LA years ago, *The Hills* was an obsession of mine. Here I was, spending my entire salary on a car I couldn't afford and fighting with men in picturesque settings. I was the gay Audrina. You know how you leave a concert and have to relive it by listening to that artist's music on the way home? Well, to highlight the drama, when I pushed the "engine off" button it also cut off One Direction's "Same Mistakes." The irony was not lost on little ol', ready to pop off me.

It started relatively calm. He explained to me that he didn't see the point of this conversation, since he knew everything he needed to. My agitation quickly escalated. Being accused of something that never happened tends to do that to a person. I remember yelling that I had never been on Grindr since moving here to find him, and how I would never betray him in that way. It was probably 1 AM and he warned me that if I kept yelling, security would probably come out. He had the nerve to act like I was making a spectacle. The spectacle creator himself was mad that I was reacting to his creation.

"You're sure it wasn't you?" he asked. "Y-e-s," I reiterated. I asked him to show me what evidence he had. He said that it wouldn't be a good idea to go there. He was completely sure that he had some evidence on me. I started believing that sure, he either stalked the Rose Bowl or had someone do it for him, and perhaps he saw someone with a profile that looked like me, but I was in no way, shape, or form on Grindr. I became nervous that over the years, maybe someone had stolen my picture and of all times, they used it at the One Direction concert. I now realize that I was so smart, I would lend my brainpower to give credence to Chris' pie in the sky allegations. This guy can't be *this* neurotic, I thought. Maybe something *did* happen and I need to explain to him that it wasn't me.

He pulled out his phone and I waited for him to show it to me. Show me the picture of myself that was going to set our relationship back yet again. He showed me the screen cap of the Grindr grid on his phone. "That's not you?" he asked, in an omniscient tone. I looked at the photo and it was actually not me. It was a picture of a guy lying on a lounge chair by a pool. All you could see were his green shorts and a Bud Light he was drinking.

"Are you fucking kidding me?" I yelled. First of all, I don't even have shorts in that color and when have you ever seen me drinking a regular Bud Light – I barely even drink. When I did drink, I was a Lime-a-Rita type bitch so I was half insulted that he knew me so little. He said that I did, in fact, have green shorts in that color because he had seen me wearing them in a recent Instagram post. I couldn't believe that our relationship had so abruptly been reduced to fighting over shades of green and social media spying. In what was possibly the gayest clapback of the year, I asked how stupid he could be to not know the difference between *my* hunter green chino shorts and this guy's aqua green board shorts.

He moved on to his next line of arguments. He showed me the guy's profile description, which said he was looking for local friends to hang out with. This did not help Chris' theory in the slightest. Everybody knows I am antisocial at my core. If I *was* on Grindr, it would be to find a date or hook up, not a damn friend. We continued to fight outside of his apartment complex. I questioned everything and accused him of lying. Lying about where he found this photo, about his cousin being at the concert. None of it added up and his answers were a bunch of diversions rerouted into new accusations against me.

Things escalated on both ends and we were both yelling. I was always more even-tempered than he, so I was shocked when he almost got physical with me. The last time I was in a fight was on the playground in 3rd grade. I don't remember what he was going to do, but he got entirely too close for comfort, as if to punch me. I was a bit rattled, but somehow felt that he had the restraint not to take it there. He probably gained even more composure when I reminded him that he probably didn't want to get physical with an almost-lawyer who had all the time in the world to call the police and unravel his professional career with restraining orders and lawsuits.

Knowing that the situation was going nowhere, I got in my car and sped off in a Spencer Pratt fashion. Two short blocks later, I was pulling into my parking garage. It was 2 AM and I still had to walk the dog after this shit. I was fuming. I had never felt so wronged by him. I wasn't sure why I was shocked since he pulled the same thing in Vegas and I managed to overlook it with time. I remember wanting to vindicate myself, even though I *knew* that *he knew* this thing was made up. He had to – since he was the one making things up all of the time.

After the dog walk, I drove about 20 minutes away to a Wal-Mart that was open all night. The law student in me was on a mission. I never thought I'd be the guy buying a case of Bud Light at Wal-Mart at 3 AM on a now Friday morning, but there I was. I rushed back home, focused on my mission, but cognizant of how annoyed I would be to add a speeding ticket to this night. I stormed into my condo as my dog looked at me. All of this commotion was throwing off his sleep equilibrium.

I went into my closet and pulled out every pair of shorts, board shorts, jeans, and pants I owned. I laid them one next to the other on my kitchen island. I opened the pack of Bud Light and placed a single can of beer on each piece of clothing. I stood back, took a picture, and texted Chris. Here was the entire collection of garments I had that donned the bottom half of my body, with a can of Bud Light against each of them. The purpose was to show Chris the color ratio between the Bud Light can and shorts in the picture as compared to a Bud Light can and my actual green shorts. I really only needed to take a picture of my green shorts and one can, but it was after 3 AM and there was no better time to be petty and include all of my pants. He texted me back fairly quickly – clearly still awake after our blowout a couple hours back. My text to him asked if he now understood that my shorts were not at all the same color as the ones the guy was wearing in the Grindr photo.

This was a colossally futile exercise, since he knew that he made up the entire thing. Similar to Vegas, I suspect that he once again came up with a plausible story to try to get me to admit to cheating.

As before, the story was blowing up in his face as his OCD and detail-oriented "boyfriend" poked apart every element of his arguments.

In the most annoying fashion, Chris responded to my text with "…filters." I exclaimed that I had not used any filters in my photo. He responded that the Grindr photo *was* in fact my green shorts, but I had filtered to make them look different. I was done. I threw my phone across the room and I was completely done. I was wasting brain cells and energy on this man. It was 4 AM and I had to be up for work in a few hours, to start the commute that I endured every day just to be near him. To be near a man that made up lies about me, insulted my intelligence, my values, and that generally drove me mad. The man that changed the course of a year-plus of my life over a few happy moments that made me desperate for more.

In taking total stock of our relationship, we had maybe 7% good times with 93% pain and suffering. This evening had finally drained me of everything. Physically, mentally, and emotionally, I had nothing left to give this situation. I gave him everything I had. I tried with every ounce to force something that I knew over a year ago was probably wrong for me. The next day was obviously no fun. My voice was hoarse, I had no energy, and my spirit was dead. I knew that a change was inevitable.

Mr. Moving On

I did not speak to Chris after the One Direction debacle. The next few weeks I fixated on how to break my lease and move away from him. I emailed the realtor who helped me rent the place. She was surprised I'd be leaving so soon and willing to pay the harsh exit penalty to do so. I remember it cost about $3,600 just to end the lease early. This was penalty money that I would never get back. I transferred it from savings, signed the papers, got a U-Haul and got the fuck out. It was money that I didn't really have, but no price was too high to move on to a better phase of my life.

I remember asking my parents to help me move. They, too, were unsure why this sudden move was happening. They were actually unsure why I moved to the area to begin with. Unfortunately, since Chris and I could not get along for more than a few days, they never would meet him or come to understand the turmoil of the past year or so. I moved to a completely different part of LA, somewhere I had never lived before and 45 minutes away from Chris. It was time to focus on school, work, and rediscover peace.

It was very difficult to move on from Chris, despite knowing that going back was not an option. It took me months just to regain sanity and not yearn for his texts to stop me from feeling lonely. I finally was back on Grindr and other apps, talking to as many guys as possible to keep me distracted. I needed to drown out the mistakes of the past couple of years. I didn't intend on finding romance or even hooking up with anyone. I just needed to keep busy. Sometimes I wonder if it's even ethical to be on dating apps in those rebound phases. Maybe our accounts should have mandatory red tags – "damaged goods" – so we don't hurt or mislead other innocent guys in our recoveries. Certainly, I have hurt others and been hurt myself in those phases.

Months later, I would get into a motorcycle accident on my way to school. It was a slightly rainy day and I succumbed to a pothole, flying off the bike and sliding down the road. The GoPro camera from Chris was not being put to use. Luckily, I was not hit by any other cars and walked away with just a few nasty scrapes. As I flew off the bike, I remember thinking "you're going to die, you're going to die, you *idiot* - why did you get a motorcycle?" Near-death moments like that make us reflect.

It was around that time that I remember making the mistake of e-mailing Chris. At this point, his number and other forms of contact were long blocked. But I always remembered his email. My brain was over him, but perhaps my heart wasn't. I remember poetically explaining to him that life is short, and perhaps our efforts to make things work were marred by our history. It should have been clear that not enough time had passed before we gave it another go. I was naïve to think that *these* few months without him were any different than the few months before I up and moved to be near him. I hated the romantic in me, romantic Lex was a masochistic idiot. I'm sure that if I had met someone remotely as captivating as Chris during this downtime, I wouldn't have thought twice about him. When you're lonely, you just go for the last best thing you had – even if it was actually pretty horrible.

I remember waiting for responses from him for probably a month. I'd send another email, here or there. Not necessarily begging for forgiveness but just pondering what we could have been now that the drama had settled. I remember Selena Gomez releasing "The Heart Wants What It Wants" around this time. That damn song resonated far too much with me. I'm not sure if this is historically accurate, but perhaps she wrote this song to justify going back to Justin Bieber even though the public hated him. It made perfect sense that I would use the same lyrics to justify going back to my personal idiot.

When you have so much time invested in someone, the easiest thing to do is to think of ways to go back and pick up where you left off. That seemed to be my recurring issue with Chris. I knew it was wrong, I knew it was difficult, and it never seemed to work, but it was a choice that I had stock in. The stock just kept dropping and I would buy more, hoping that it would bounce back and my entire investment would be justified. But it didn't come back and it wasn't coming back. The company had tanked. I guess when I moved to be near Chris I knew the "company" was failing, but thought a new location or logo would help us out. I tried to rebrand Blockbuster. I was dating the DVD of gay men and everyone was looking at me like, "bitch you don't stream?"

Eventually, Chris replied to one of my emails. This was maybe 9 months after I had moved away. With time, I wore him out with romantic ideals. I'm positive that he had nothing else going on in his dating life and perhaps that's why he replied. He always found it endearing that I wouldn't give up on him. It's funny how he thought that someone who was writing him loving emails to months of no response was the same type of person to allegedly betray him by cruising on Grindr at a One Direction concert.

His response was hesitant, at best. We both claimed to have changed with time and to be leading relatively boring lifestyles. Work, school, home. Weeks later, we would meet on the basis of friendship at a Coffee Bean. Not *our* Coffee Bean, thank God. That would be too sentimental, even for me. By this point, I remembered hoping that if he couldn't be my man, perhaps he could just be my friend and I wouldn't have to lose him. In the investing analogy, I guess our partnership had gone under but I now had some money and was asking to purchase our branding rights to hold onto if they ever became valuable again. I guess I just wanted to keep my eye on him, in case. In case of what, I'm not sure. There was nothing about us that worked, but I still had love for the asshole.

He showed up to the new Coffee Bean and my heart skipped a beat. He was as cute as he had always been. He bought my drink and cookie. We spoke distantly, but in a generally positive manner. We were navigating the new normal and what we were allowed to say to one another. The topics were pretty neutral. I still knew how to make him laugh, just like the first time we met. I had slight hope that, with time, we would be able to sustain a distant friendship. Perhaps that would make me feel like the whole thing wasn't a complete waste.

Before we left that day, he told me about a Mercedes he had ordered. Since I loved cars, I asked him about it at length. He wasn't prepared for this. He told me the model of the car and the year. I told him that what he was saying couldn't be correct. This was around the time that Mercedes was redoing their model naming scheme. Chris liked cars, but did not know as much as me. He told me that he was probably confused about the naming, but he was doing a European delivery of the car and making a vacation out of it.

I congratulated him on the car, which was a six-figure model that solidified to me he must be doing pretty well these days.

We didn't talk very frequently after this meeting. A text here or there. We both seemed to be going along with the friendship vibes, and I was getting comfortable with that reality. I had managed to do this with my first ex. We would see each other a few times throughout the year to hike or grab dinner, and it felt better than completely losing him in my life. Chris never liked that arrangement with my first ex, but he never liked anything at all.

About a month later, I texted Chris to ask how the European delivery of his Mercedes went. He said it was a lot of fun. I asked to see a picture of the car. He said he would have to look for one. As car guys, asking for a picture of your car is like asking a parent for a picture of their child. They definitely have one, especially if their child cost over $100,000. After a little back and forth, Chris "found a picture" of the car and sent it to me. It was a pretty blurry picture of the car on a mountain road. I asked why his phone would take such a blurry picture and he made up some excuse about it being windy when he took it.

I mentioned that the model in this photo was in fact the Mercedes with the new naming scheme, which was not what he told me he was buying. He tried to correct me by saying the car was actually under the old naming scheme. I started to become bothered with this, wondering if Chris was lying to me yet again. I was a bit weary that he would be buying such an expensive car anyway, but over the years had figured out that he had a rich family and would pretend to be more independent that he perhaps truly was. I believed that he could find a way to buy such a car, but the story wasn't adding up.

I sent him screen caps of the Mercedes website, what the new model is named and looks like, what the old model was named and looked like. He stuck to his story. I began negotiating his lies for him again. I offered that perhaps since he did a European delivery, the model was manufactured one year prior to the U.S. release of the vehicle and got misclassified by customs. This would be the only way his story added up. I asked him to show me the registration on the car. He would not. Later that night, something told me to run the picture of the car he sent me through a reverse Google search. The same picture came up numerous times linked to a Chinese website which had taken a picture of the car in its testing phase.

I showed him the Chinese website with his supposed mountain drive picture and asked why he lied. He denied it and we never spoke again. He had gotten under my skin one last time. It seems that even when we were just being friends, he had the ability to tell me stone cold lies, knowing how much I cared for and valued him. Even with the multiple false Grindr accusations of the years, I knew he was lying. This was the first time, however, that I had hard and blatant evidence of his lying to shove in his face.

As upset as I was, I felt vindicated. All of my agonizing over proving his lies over the years finally boiled to the surface. He so sloppily lied about something so stupid to me. Was he trying to impress me with his life? Was he trying to fuck with me? Did he actually still believe that I lied to him over the years and was this his way of getting me back? I never understood why Chris told this final lie. It was ultimately a blessing. Writing this now, over four years later, I still have never spoken to Chris again. I remember he found me on Instagram once and tried to send me a message that I denied. "Long time no talk, I've been meaning to call you." Reject.

I would see him on Tinder here or there. He would always be using the same pictures from years ago. It saddened me that he put so little effort into his own dating life. My heart would always skip a beat when he came up. There he is – I wondered whose life he would ruin next. I would look at him for a second and swipe left, shaking my head. Every relationship runs its course. Ours had gone up and down, starting and ending numerous times. But when you know something is done, it is truly done. I think that happens when your heart and your mind agree that it is over. Those two had never agreed about Chris before now, but thankfully, they finally did.

[3] WHAT CHRIS TAUGHT ME

I could honestly write an entire book, separate from *The Grid*, on the extensive list of lessons I learned from my tumultuous relationship with Chris. The rapper Eve once said, "love is blind, and it'll take over your mind." And that is literally all I have to say about Chris and his trifling ass.

Half joking. I think a recurrent theme with Chris was that of mental and emotional abuse. It is striking to me, even now, just how much I allowed myself to go through with Chris. Note – *allowed* myself. Despite my many issues and criticisms of Chris, a person can only be as abusive to you as you allow them to be. I could have walked away from Chris many times, but chose not to. That said, the abuse is striking because I considered myself fairly smart and confident during my time with Chris. I knew that I was a catch; I knew that I had a lot to offer someone, and I repeatedly bent over backwards to offer it to Chris.

I think about the stereotypical rhetoric around abuse, however, and feel that maybe I shouldn't be surprised. I think of people saying, "she's such a pretty girl, doesn't she know she can do better?" "Why does she put up with that loser – can't she find someone else?" It is clear to me that a victim of abuse isn't necessarily someone lacking self-esteem. While I imagine that those who suffer from self-esteem issues deal with a fair share of abuse, I truly feel that it can happen to anyone.

Perhaps love is the elixir that nulls self-esteem, confidence, and common sense. It makes us drunk enough to think that we are in love with a person who, in the whole, is detracting from our happiness and putting us through constant drama and pain. I think the core of my issues with Chris was just that. I was willing to put up with just about anything he did to me because I loved him. As time passed, that love continued and I would go deeper and deeper into a hole I couldn't get myself out of. It was self-perpetuating, I would recognize the hell that I was going through but would continue to try because of the amount of time I had put into him. Logically, as time passed, we had more and more issues. So the idea that I should continue trying using the theory of "time invested" dragged the problem along endlessly.

Chris constantly made me question values in myself that I never questioned before. On more occasions than even described he questioned my loyalty, dedication, seriousness, and honesty. Through facts slowly and later learned, I knew that he was turning many of his problems outwardly against me. It's almost as though he was making me suffer through a lifetime of abuses he had faced himself. While I don't blame him for the abuses he experienced out of his control, I wish that he had the foresight to know that he would constantly be using them against me in a relationship. We all have pasts and I am sympathetic to all abuse. If Chris were serious about me, I would have gladly gone to therapy or spoken to a professional about the best way to maintain our relationship and be cognizant of his (and my own) issues. Therapy before marriage – how romantic. But seriously, that's how invested I was. Chris made me feel crazy. It was no wonder, because multiple times he literally created lies to test my reactions in an attempt to confirm his own insecurities about us. Over time, his tactics made me feel insecure about myself. This was also something that had never been a real issue for me before.

What I take away from these themes of love, mental abuse, accusations, and insecurity is this: despite my intense love of Chris, I knew the entire time something did not feel right with him. Most people cannot turn this self-awareness off, no matter how in love they are. In fact, this gut feeling of something potentially wrong is why humans fight with one another. When something doesn't align – when something the other says doesn't make sense – we question and sometimes argue with the other person. No matter who is right in those arguments, it should signal to you that something is not meshing.

Now…I'm not saying to give up on a relationship that has arguments. They all do, and honey, you will never find a man with that amount of self-righteousness. But I will say that when the arguments are constant, and when the themes of the arguments are consistent, it should signal to you that something is wrong. One or both of you are not changing or adapting to a behavior causing the recurring arguments. That lack of compromise spells failure for most relationships in the long term.

This is exactly what happened to Chris and me. The subject matter of the arguments may have been different, but the issues were consistently clear to me. He was insecure about so many things and taking them out on me. He was using minor incidents that most people wouldn't think twice about to build cases against me that I would have to disprove over our entire relationship. I knew this and felt that something was wrong every time. I discussed much of this with my friends. I often shared with them just how ridiculous my relationship with him was. But I kept going back. Earlier, I quoted Eve. Perhaps love is not completely blind, however. Perhaps love is a very, very dark lens on a pair of sunglasses. You absolutely see what is happening and how it looks and feels wrong to you, but you try to filter out that light as much as possible. I am not qualified to speak on abuse in every circumstance, and perhaps it is very different for others, but this is what I extract from my years with Chris.

My advice here would be not to ignore what you see in your own relationships. You have a heart and a brain for two different reasons. One is romance and one is logic. Strike the fine balance between both, but don't let one take over. My heart took over with Chris. I could hear my brain screaming constantly that he was wrong for me, but my heart would continually press mute on my brain to get what it wanted.

I also encourage all of you to bounce ideas off of your family, friends, or anyone that knows you well and has your best interest at heart. My friends constantly reaffirmed to me that my experiences with Chris were not normal and that he seemed like, for lack of a better word, an asshole. They pointed out to me, gently, but consistently that our relationship was toxic. I heard every word they said on the many occasions they said it. Perhaps my heart was attempting to put them on mute as well, but I think those were important conversations and reminders to have. Perhaps, with time, they rang loud enough to partially encourage me to make a change. No matter what your situation is, remember that the people closest to you do not want to see you hurt. And whether you take their advice or not, it is good to listen to them completely and get outside perspectives often when it comes to problematic relationships. As you can see, it is quite easy to be blind to the fact that you may be in a horrible situation and forgetful of how you deserve the complete opposite.

Another prominent theme with Chris is the idea of manipulation. From start to finish, our relationship was full of it. I think of our early conversations and the pressure he put on me to come out to my family. Rather than encourage me on my coming out journey, or even congratulate me for the extent to which I had come out already, Chris used the fact that I wasn't fully out as a form of manipulation. If I wanted to be serious with him, it had to happen - and soon. Considering how early in our relationship he made this request, I feel that he could have been much more sympathetic, or even helpful as to how to go about it.

He set the tone early to make me feel that his love and attention were fleeting, and I would need to continually meet his expectations to keep him around. There's a difference between conversations about needs versus setting all-or-nothing demands on your partner. I believe a healthy relationship focuses more on conversations, understanding your partner's backstory, their wishes, and their plans for the future. If I could do it over, I would want a partner to walk me through the benefits of coming out to my family. I would want them to tell me they would be as patient as necessary, but that it was important to them. I wouldn't want to feel like I had to do it or they would leave me. I still thank Chris now for the pressure, because I am now fully out and I didn't actually see that vision for myself so early, but the manipulative approach reeked of abuse.

This manipulation continued. I think back to the New Year's when we weren't having a good time and he guilted me into sex. "It's New Years Eve, I'm 28 and in a sexless relationship." I can hear his words now. I wish I said what I felt in that moment rather than appease him. Something like, "maybe it wouldn't be sexless if you were a decent, non-abusive, compassionate, and fair type of bitch." Sex and intimacy is something that should always be mutual and enjoyable. If you are having sex out of guilt with someone or if any aspect of your intimacy seems forced, step back and evaluate your situation. Do not give the most intimate aspect of your being to someone who doesn't make you feel like it's valued.

I can go on endlessly about the manipulation with Chris – one standout includes when I broke up with him because he stopped talking to me, and how he branded me a cheater for the rest of our relationship because I made a new Grindr account. Another is when we fought, I kicked him out of my apartment, and he claimed to get robbed at gunpoint. Chris was very good at turning situations where he had some wrongdoing completely against me and making me feel bad indefinitely. It was a form of gaslighting – making me question my own sanity regarding clear-cut situations.

I encourage all of you to examine your relationships for manipulation. A clear sign to me is if your partner continues to bring up past events, accusing you of some wrongdoing. If those past events have already been discussed and resolved, it is not productive to keep rehashing them in the relationship. If your partner continues to use them against you, I consider this an unhealthy form of manipulation. It's like saying, "although I forgave you, I will use this as a tool to make you feel bad as needed for the rest of our relationship." It's manipulative and unproductive – it's not what people in love do to one another. Additionally, it is completely bad for the mental health of the receiving person. It makes you feel like a consistent failure, and unworthy of your partner's love. In my case, where I felt that I had actually done nothing wrong, it made me feel like I constantly had to prove myself or make something up to Chris. It was a mind fuck, to say the least.

What repeatedly did me in with Chris were feelings of loneliness. This is much more a personal issue than an issue with what Chris was doing. In fact, this is an issue I dealt with literally today, as I write this. I feel that Grindr and dating app culture is a drug that came with no warning. Most of us have been hooked for years without even realizing. Need proof? Try having Grindr for a month and then deleting Grindr for a month. Some of you may have exceptional self-control, but many of you know the constant feelings of picking up your phone and going to click an app that isn't there. It's like an Instagram addiction but with your heart (or penis?) – the stakes are much higher. The loneliness without Grindr stems from the constant and instant stream of attention it provides. Over the years, we become very used to that attention.

No matter where you are in the world, opening Grindr will provide a familiar grid of the 100 closest gay men (or more, for you ballers on Grindr Xtra). The familiarity and accessibility of that grid gives you a feeling of community. Even if you're on a road trip in the middle of nowhere, you can open that app and quench your loneliness. If the closest gay person to you is 20 miles away, you still feel like you have someone right there to talk to. You can refresh your screen every 30 seconds in a moving vehicle and have a seemingly endless array of men to talk to. This technologically driven reality is a false one. We get used to constantly talking to someone to fulfill our sexual and romantic needs, and we lose our sense of reality and the ability to survive alone. So many of us find ourselves deleting Grindr, emboldened to find a man the "right way." "I want to find dick at the Trader Joe's," a guy once told me. I think I responded, how do you know the Trader Joe's dick doesn't also have Grindr? He suggested that it was different – it was classier to meet at Trader Joe's. It's more elegant to tell your friends he was shopping for eggplant, rather than cruising for eggplant. Perhaps so, but the reality for me is that it is very difficult to deal with a life without apps.

In a way, the apps provide safety and convenience. Many of us may prefer to approach and speak to men in our day to day lives, but it can be intimidating and even scary to know which ones are gay or even open to being approached. The last thing you want to do is get hurt by a drunk straight man who you thought was giving you the "flirt stare," rather than the "death stare." The apps give us that filter to feel comfortable and approach only the men who are open to it. I thank Grindr and similar apps whole-heartedly for giving us this tool. In a way, Grindr has equipped so many of us to meet men, have experiences and discover parts of ourselves that we never would have if we didn't have it as a tool.

I imagine a life without Grindr, and when (if ever) I would feel comfortable meeting or dating men. I guess I would spend a lot more time in the gay neighborhoods or clubs. I'm certain the generation before Grindr made it work somehow. Despite these positive aspects of Grindr, I do hold it (and perhaps, more broadly, technology and social media) responsible for making us feel a complete void and loneliness without it. Had I not been so hooked to constant attention when it came to dating, I am confident that I would not have convinced myself to go back to Chris so many times. I think the Grindr generation has trained many of us to feel that romantic and sexual attention should be constant, when it was far less frequent before the advent of these apps. Imagine how much work it would be to talk to as many guys as we do on Grindr in a week, in real life, without technology.

My lesson here is that we, as individuals, need to take responsibility over our own actions in preventing addiction to apps like Grindr. Grindr is not our mom, and it's not going to tell us to stop playing video games and to go to bed. By keeping your app use in check, I firmly believe you will lead a much healthier and balanced life, have greater perspective and self-awareness, and make fewer mistakes in dating out of desperation and loneliness. My tips for anyone who wants to wean off of Grindr – give yourself a realistic timeline. If you have been hooked for years, try not using it for a day or two. Stick to your timeline. Work yourself up to a week, or even a month. Maybe even try a week-on and week-off schedule. This will curb your use. A related, and important step is to replace the time you would have sat around on Grindr to do something productive. Read a book (may I suggest *The Grid* – and tell your friends to read it too), go to the gym, get outside, and hang out with the friends you've been neglecting. If you have no replacement activity for using the apps, it is going to be hard to stay off of them. Also, it doesn't hurt to do things that are good for you!

Finally, my tip is to tell a friend or have someone hold you accountable to your Grindr breaks. Tell someone that you will not be using it for a month – if they catch you, tell them to slap you. Whatever you have to do to keep your app use in check will benefit you in the long run. When I'm in a relationship I don't think twice about Grindr. It's not the app itself or the random nudes that keep me coming – it's the simple need of wanting attention and love from another man. The single periods of my life are what make it difficult. If we keep our Grindr check in use, perhaps we all can do a better job of surviving without letting loneliness take over.

Another "a-ha," or rather, "duh bitch," moment from my relationship with Chris is the idea of putting more effort into someone than they put into you. This is pretty obvious, but it was a theme that I seemingly ignored with Chris. One shining example of this was the fact that Chris never let me see his apartment after we became boyfriends, and yet, I was willing to move when he left the city and signed a lease to live right next to him. I was clearly putting in a bit more effort in the "convenience of sharing our home lives" department. My thought here is that, while a relationship should never be tit-for-tat or perfectly equal, you should take note (or listen to your friends take note) of you doing far more than your partner does for you.

All relationships have give and take, and some of the best relationships have one partner give in a certain way with the other returning something completely different. This give and take might even come in seasons. Perhaps one partner gives more while the other is in school, or going through a life change, etc. But it ultimately should be mutual and balance out. Please do not convince yourself, like I did, that continuing to give more to someone who already isn't matching you will make it better. You are likely just digging a deeper hole for yourself. My suggestion to those of you who feel like your partner is not mutually giving to the relationship is to have a conversation. Tell them your concerns and let them know how it makes you feel to be in an uneven situation. If, after that conversation, you are unable to come to a consensus, I would evaluate whether or not continuing in the relationship feels fair to you. Do not go rogue and just have blind faith that someone will change or improve. If I could do it all over again with Chris, I would have a lot more of these conversations and his responses would likely have signaled to me that he just did not give a fuck in the same way that I did. If a man constantly signals to you that he doesn't value you, believe him and move on.

With that comes my final warning from my relationship with Chris. Do not allow competition or jealousy to take over your relationships. I think back to the phase in which Chris and I were surprising one another with gifts, almost trying to one-up one another to show who cared more by spending the most. I think for gay people in particular, the threat of a competitive partner is very real. Perhaps it's because our relationships eschew gender norms, such as chivalry, where a woman might expect a man to be a gentleman and pay for her dinner, or buy her Valentine's Day gifts. In a gay relationship, that traditional pressure is not on one particular partner. This competition can also relate closely to jealousy. I have had relationships where my partner or I have admitted to jealousy or competition in our careers, salaries, or even shallow things like the cars we drove. While jealousy and competition are natural human traits, I believe that they have a very small place in romantic relationships. If you are in a relationship that constantly makes you or your partner feel these ways, you should have a serious conversation on how to avoid creating any feelings of competition.

With Chris, I wish I could go back and tell him that the gift giving was a beautiful gesture, but perhaps we should limit them to $10 gifts that took the competitive financial pressure off, allowing the gesture of thoughtfulness to remain. At the end of the day, jealousy and competition will exist, but should not be a stress or controlling factor in your relationships. As gay people, I think we need to remain extra conscious of these threats to our romantic lives. We deal with enough jealousy following Instagram models, at work, at school, and in many other facets of our lives. Our relationships should be sacred temples of solitude, where none of that shit matters and we can be ourselves without those worries. Find a partner that makes you feel at ease, not competitive or jealous.

I remember in one of our many break ups, Chris was being petty and asked for all of his gifts back (see: section on manipulation). I told him that he should never give gifts if he expected them back and that it was so trashy of him to do so. Using that theme, I put all of the fancy gifts he bought me in a large trash bag, met him at *our* Coffee Bean, dropped the bag on his feet, and drove off as he cried in my rearview mirror. That particular image of Chris is comforting to me after all of the garbage he ultimately put me through.

[4] LESSON TWO: TYLER

It was in my first year of law school. Most people quit their jobs that first year of school to put their entire focus on their new endeavor. School was no joke, but I was used to juggling a lot. No matter how much I focused on my studies, there was still that empty few hours in the evenings when I would be glued to my phone, scrolling through the familiar Grindr grid. I remember that this was a particularly fruitless period on the grid; it was a lot of nothing. Many guys were not answering my "hi plus picture" messages, each one bringing my self-esteem down a notch. The guys I did talk to for a bit would be quick conversations, nothing of substance. It would continue like this for months. I wasn't big on hooking up via Grindr in this phase, so perhaps I shouldn't have expected much from an app built with that in mind. Since I did have some prior dates and positive experiences from Grindr, here I was, scrolling with a glimmer of hope for love.

Back in this time (still before Tinder), there was really no other way to meet gay guys aside from going to the clubs or risking walking up to a guy who might be gay in real life, accompanied with the fear that he might kill you if he's not. I personally found gay clubs extremely intimidating and full of guys who were not my type. No offense to those who enjoy them, but they were always in a part of town far away from me, and the guys in attendance seemed to be the "advanced gay" set. I was out here searching for my first gay experiences. I was talking baby steps, and the clubs were a gay leap I wasn't ready for. I feel that by using Grindr, I was using the most viable option for me to meet potentially quality gay men at the time. I always figured, if I am on here, someone like me must also be in the same situation.

Southern Surprise

It was about 11 PM on a Monday night when I messaged Tyler. He was less than a mile away from me and I was surprised that I hadn't seen him before. He was 29 and I was about 22 at this time. I remember that he was just as tall as me, which is hard and exciting to find at 6'2". These early days were when I first discovered my complex around gay dating and height. The gay dating pool has a laundry list of innocent preferences – and also horrible microaggressions *disguised* as preferences. On the innocent end of the spectrum could be things like a guy's location and style – on the horrible end would be racism, fem shaming, and body shaming. I struggle with where height preferences fall on this spectrum. It's obviously something a person cannot change about themselves, which makes me feel a bit horrible for having a preference about it. On the other hand, it's not necessarily a trait that has years of documented prejudicial treatment behind it.

Initially, I never thought height would matter to me. After meeting and hooking up with men much shorter than me, however, I realized I had some internal issues about how my partner's height made me feel. For instance, if I was much taller than him and he had to look up to kiss me, I clicked into a weird "whoa this is probably how it feels if a girl kisses me" mode, most women being shorter than 6'2". To be clear, the issue is on my end. I actually wish I was shorter because I have probably already categorically denied the man of my dreams for being 5'5". I *will* say that you cannot control who you are physically attracted to, and you will drive yourself crazy if you hyper-analyze all of your preferences. It's hard enough to find a man as it is. That said, it is never ok to be an asshole about expressing your preferences online, as they can truly make others feel horrible for traits they cannot change about themselves. Not to mention that obviously things like racism, fem shaming, and body shaming (among others) are intolerable – period. With time, I have loosened my height standards and I hope I can get over that complex altogether on my end.

Back to Tyler. He had beautiful dirty blonde hair, styled perfectly in his picture. There was a refinement in how he presented himself. He didn't look like anyone I had dated before, and I think it excited me to experience a new flavor of man, if you will. I remember he quickly responded to my "hi plus picture" message, which I was not expecting at all, let alone that late at night. As the old gay adage goes, if he's *your* type, you're never his honey.

But Tyler surprisingly disproved that. I could immediately tell he was smart and attentive, two of my weaknesses. We messaged until about 3 AM that night. I didn't see that coming at all. We talked about where we grew up – he was from the South, I was local LA trash. I learned that he was in the entertainment industry in a behind-the-scenes kind of way. He had his own business that seemed to be doing well, and he was definitely independent. We talked about both of our love of cars, which almost never happens in the gay world.

It was very easy to talk to him, and he had quickly captivated my full attention. Despite all of your friends and family, there's something about talking to a new love interest that makes it feel like they're the only person you want to talk to and share everything with. You're inspired to catch them up on multiple decades of your life, share old stories, old photos. It's the "let me tell you everything about me so we can be each other's everything" phase. Although night one is premature for those types of thoughts, I was feeling that excitement with Tyler. Something was happening and we both knew it.

I always wonder if those rare yet amazing conversations on Grindr only appear to be amazing because of the comparative bullshit you're dealing with on the app. Is this guy really perfect or do I just have an extremely low standard for men after being on this thing? Regardless, in the moment, you are willing to accept any attention being given to you. The next morning, I remember waking up to get ready for school and Tyler being the first thing on my mind. I texted him and he quickly responded. This is always an important test - the "next day" test. Were we both just really lonely and desperate last night or do we still like each other enough to respond to texts before lunch? I was pretty excited to have my new "priority penis" to text.

Most single gay men have a couple of go-to guys on their roster that they hit up here and there, but when you are truly excited about someone, they jump to the top of your list. Tyler had taken his spot at #1 overnight. Not only was he pretty damn great, but he also had little competition because everyone sucked so much at this time. I remember texting him throughout class. Thankfully Apple added iMessage to Macbooks so you could keep the texting going through your insufferable Criminal Law class. He was working and I was in school, but the conversation kept flowing consistently. After this continued back and forth, we decided that I would go over to his place downtown after my final class that afternoon. Despite liking him, I remember being a bit hesitant meeting him at his house for the first time rather than a restaurant or coffee shop. Around this time, I was going through an "I ride my bike to school because I am urban chic" phase, so I wasn't eager to bike all the way to Tyler's part of the city. Nonetheless, class ended and I made my way downtown to his building. Did any of us have a doubt that I would?

Dick and the City

I remember texting him that I had arrived and for him to come down and get me. He texted back asking me to come through the front and have security buzz me up. I remember thinking "hell no." Normally I would take a certain number of risks, but Grindr is full of sketchy men. I wasn't trying to be the cute law student that got killed on a Grindr run meeting a damn stranger in his downtown loft. I told him he needed to come downstairs or I would not be seeing him. He thought I was joking, but I wasn't. It freaked me out that he was so unwilling to come downstairs to get me. I remember almost turning my bike around and heading home before he told me he was on his way down. It's going to be a catfish for sure, I thought. Who would have such a problem with coming down to meet me and make me feel comfortable?

Eventually he came outside, looking even better than his pictures. "What the fuck?" I remember thinking, as my heart skipped a beat. You know that rare feeling when you meet someone and they are actually better looking than you were prepared for? I just showed up looking like little ol' me, and you want to be all sexy and smiling, ready to spend time with me? I still had reservations about the coming downstairs debacle, but together we went back to his place. He told me it was just more convenient to buzz people up, he had it set up that way. I thought, well ok, that's not going to work for the first time you meet me sweetheart. I don't care how pretty you are.

He opened the door to his place and I remember being instantly impressed. It was a beautiful two-story historical loft in the heart of downtown. This guy had great taste. To a young gay man, there's something infinitely impressive about a guy in his late twenties or thirties who can afford the Restoration Hardware you desire but are in no way prepared to buy. That rang true for every older man I've dated. They all had such good taste, nice pieces of furniture, the stuff you wouldn't think to get in your early years. Fancy bathroom décor. Candles. The nicer bath towels from Target that your cheap ass always skips. Their houses always smelled good. I just hope that my current décor makes others feel the same way. I hope I am doing the late-20's gay scene justice in my interior design taste level. But, 1 digress.

I remember thinking this guy had good taste – from his furniture to his clothes. I set my bike alongside his wall, and it instantly blended into his urban décor. I put my backpack down and cautiously sat on one of his leather accent chairs in a "now what" kind of way. The conversation was a bit awkward for those first 10 minutes. I remember still being a little freaked out after that "buzz me up" incident. I guess I was still waiting for him to pull out a knife and kill me. But Tyler wasn't that guy, thankfully.

We bantered a bit back and forth, and frankly, I couldn't tell what direction it was going. The conversation was unlike the rapid back and forth excitement on Grindr the night prior. This is an ongoing theme and fear of mine in meeting people online. It's so easy to build an image of a person via text messaging and pictures that is completely unlike the human on the other end of the phone. That is why I always try to meet people in real life fairly quickly after the initial exchange of messages. I don't want to fall in love with an idea of someone that doesn't exist; that had happened to me too many times before. The exchange of "what would I do without you" and "I love you" by day 5 of texting, then meeting in real life and asking a practical stranger for those words back.

In a way, it's a good thing that apps can't completely replicate humanity. That combination of a person's voice, eyes, laughs, scent…these are all things that require a human in front of you. So here was a human in front of me, and I was beginning to fear I had built a false image in my head. I'm not sure what wasn't connecting – perhaps we were both nervous. All of the questions seemed to be a dead end and wouldn't flow into deeper conversation. I can take some of the blame on that as I tend to close up when I feel weird about a situation. Let this be a warning – if you actually like someone, try not to be too judgmental of how they act on the first date. So many people are nervous and take a while to warm up, and those early judgments can have you losing out on a great person.

I think we liked each other too much at this point to let it fail. We awkward bantered for about an hour before he asked if I was hungry. I figured, he hasn't killed me yet and the conversation isn't amazing so I might as well check dinner off of my list. We made our way to get some Mexican take-out. I left my bike at his place. I guess that said it all. We went down into his parking garage and I found my way into his truck. This was rare for LA, I was expecting a Prius or something. A truck really did wonders for his image of being some kind of Southern gentleman.

I think the real appeal of a truck to me is that it is something I would never drive, so it feels different and cool - dare I say, impressive. Perhaps years of conditioning, advertising, and movies make us associate trucks with masculinity. I do find masculinity attractive, but abrasive masculinity is actually a turn off to me. I don't want to be afraid of or threatened by your maleness. I guess I am ok with masculinity so long as it is drowning in sensitivity, has a sweet disposition, and knows the words to "I'm A Slave 4 U." It's similar to tolerating tomatoes in salads, but only when soaked in ranch. Tyler was a tomato dripping in ranch, and I was here to tolerate honey.

We pulled up in our truck, ordered our food, and made it back to his loft. I remember this whole process being especially cute and exciting. To someone who is perpetually single, running errands with another person feels new and fun. I remember thinking this is how it could be every weeknight! Coming home from school, talking, eating together. Companionship with someone you enjoy – imagine that! Several little things Tyler did along the way sealed the deal. He opened my car door and the restaurant door. He paid for my food. He really made me feel like a lady. Our conversation hadn't been amazing in person, but these little gestures were really making me like him. I don't remember if we even started our meal before we found ourselves making out on his couch. We made out for literally an hour.

It was new and amazing. It was the perfect storm of elements that made it so: his beauty, his chivalry, the sexy downtown backdrop. This was the best connection I had made in a long time.

That make out session was also perfect because it was the kind that knew its limits. Call me a prude, but I have much more appreciation for a make out that is simply a make out rather than the mandatory "make out but I want to have sex in a few minutes" kind. Just when it was going too far, he would back off and readjust. He was really just appreciating and enjoying me. We ended that make out session on an overpriced rug adorning the concrete floors of that loft. What the fuck was this? An artsy deep cut on the Netflix LGBT section?

Without much coaxing, Tyler convinced me to spend the night at the loft with him. This was the first time I had accepted such an offer from a guy I had met the same day. Perhaps it was because we hadn't had sex so I would never come to my senses that evening (if you know what I mean.) I figured, my bike is already here and I'm damn sure not riding home at this hour. Also, this man is perfect. I stayed and we maintained our innocence that night. It was just nice to be with him in his space. As a side note, talk about the passion and fun I was having in life before I got my dog! This would never work today because I always have to go home and walk the sucker.

Unfortunately, I woke up to the reality that it was another weekday. I had school, and I didn't exactly finish my rigorous Contracts Law reading the night prior. I told him I had to wake up early to finish my homework. Ladies – let this be a lesson to you. You always need to put that degree before that dick. That's why I'm writing this book at a Starbucks as a lawyer, and well, read on for what happens between Tyler and me. Tyler continued to be exceedingly sweet the morning after. He let me start my reading and ran to Starbucks to get an iced coffee for me. He was so immensely sweet and thoughtful. Finally, he drove my bike and me to my house (that truck came in handy), and I got ready for my day at school. This guy was a complete keeper.

Best Thing I Never Had

Things went exceedingly well with Tyler for weeks. I learned more about his interests, his passion for the company he had started. He was an amazing texter. This was particularly important to me as I spent most of my days withering away in classes. We spent a ton of time together and started doing weekend activities. We would go on hikes; we would go to the beach and just talk. He always appreciated our mutual love of cars and would try to incorporate that into his dates.

One moment that stands out is when he took me to the LA Auto Show. Around this time, I was very into an automotive Tumblr blog I had so I was taking a lot of pictures at the show to post online. I noticed Tyler starting to take pictures too. At one point I said, "that's a bad angle to take a car picture." He responded that he wasn't taking a picture of the car. He was taking a picture of me taking a picture of the car. He said it was beautiful to him to capture my passion for something. I thought that was such a sweet sentiment. This guy really cared about my passions and me. He remembered details and he made an effort to cherish moments with me. Tyler was a romantic and I had yet to experience that in a gay dating scene seemingly focused on sex, all day, every day, and in every way.

I slowly began to tell all of my friends about Tyler. Everyone I told about him loved the sound of him. It's hard not to love a guy taking such a keen and romantic interest in one of your friends. To this day, my friends reflect fondly on Tyler. Unfortunately, they have to reflect because they never met Tyler before I made the decision to leave him.

I hope my readers have expressed a collective "bitch what?" Well, I'm with you. It was a very difficult decision to leave the most perfect man I had met at that point in my life. Unfortunately, despite such a strong chemistry and romantic connection, my conversations with Tyler were never quite deep. Those lulls in conversation from our very first date never improved much. Although we had a deep interest in one another and clearly were attracted, we would often run out of things to talk about. Our conversations were always quite surface level. Our mutual attraction and, particularly, my attraction to Tyler's romantic and gentlemanly qualities are likely what kept us going. Unfortunately, I feel this happens quite often in gay dating. We have such low standards for men that the first one who is pretty good is often confused for "perfect," as we sweep potential issues under the rug to hopefully resolve themselves.

I guess the conversation seemed so exciting that first night on Grindr because we had a lot of ground to cover. We were rattling off all of our interests and expressing how cute the other was. But that's just a sharing of histories. Once we learned all of those things about one another, we didn't have much else to say. I remember awkwardly quiet dinners. I guess for me, I needed a deeper mental connection. To discuss more than the things we did that day. I wanted to discuss world events or hypothetical spiritual theories.

Our mental connection became boring and I made the extremely difficult decision to let Tyler know. He was quite surprised and seemed a bit broken over it. Perhaps he thought it was a cop out for some other reason. I knew that letting go of Tyler would mean going back to the Grindr cesspool. I would be going back to a world of unsolicited nudes and conversations even emptier than the so-called problematic ones with Tyler. I knew I would be worse off, but something did not feel right so I broke it off. I regretted it for months, and as assumed, I remained alone for months.

As difficult as it was to be alone, I felt a small sense of pride by not settling in my relationships. It felt good not to need someone out of fear of being alone. Over the years, however, I learned that there was a difference between not settling and not trying. It's good not to accept something that isn't right for you, but I typically did not put in much effort or work into making things better before walking away. Perhaps Grindr was to blame for that. Although I just described it as a cesspool, it was also conveniently an endless sea of men to choose from that made it easy to walk away from marginally inconvenient situations. Whether the waters of Grindr were blue or toxic green, they were vast. The instant gratification of Grindr's vastness certainly played a part in how hard I tried (or didn't) to make things work in relationships.

I Want You Back-ish

As most of know, loneliness has a way of revising history to seem more positive than it really was. Those months without Tyler had me thinking about him often. I thought about whether I had copped out, and wondered how bad the problem really was. I left a man for a problem – slightly boring conversations – that was much better than my current situation – absolutely no conversations. Over time, I convinced myself that I had not given Tyler a proper chance. This seemed to be a common theme not only in my life but also the stories of gay dating I often hear about.

Because the "good" guys are so few and far between, unless you move to a new city or have some major life change, you find yourself thinking about the good guys from your past quite often. That thinking culminates into texting them back, asking to hang out, being "just friends," and ultimately wanting to take another stab at the relationship. I wonder if this is attributable to there being so few gay people to begin with, leaving us with fewer relevant options to choose from. Or perhaps we form stronger attachments to the guys we have found some success with, since successful gay relationships seem so rare and coveted. Nonetheless, I found myself texting Tyler asking how he had been, with the ultimate goal of getting back into his life.

To Tyler's credit, he was quite apprehensive of my coming back around. This is probably testament to how surprisingly and quickly I seemed to be over him months before. It became clear that he was not dating anyone new, but would have to proceed cautiously with me because he didn't want to be hurt again. I felt that this was fair and we should approach the situation anew, trying to find more commonalities and establish a deeper connection. There's something so special (and weird) about the first time you see someone from your past. It's almost like they're always slightly cuter than you remembered. Nostalgia has a way to beat a man for the gods.

I remember seeing Tyler and instantly questioning how the hell I left such a seemingly ideal person. Our environment was slightly different, Tyler had given up the downtown lifestyle for a simpler place in an LA suburb. I remember sitting on his still stunning leather couch in what seemed to be an environment unfit for it. He was making some changes in his business so perhaps he was simplifying his lifestyle. Though tentative, he seemed happy to see me. We struggled through an awkward 30 first minutes, buffered by some *Dancing with the Stars* in the background. I hated this show, but it gave us some things to point out and laugh at, lightening the mood.

The good thing about Tyler's new place was that it had a little yard. I was able to take my newly acquired dog over and let him run around. This was a novel phenomenon in or around LA. I remember being excited that both my dog and I were welcome, and potentially could stay the night without the drama of when to go home. I remember we even took my dog to the local dog park on one of these occasions. Tyler and I seemed to like these types of activities, easily allowing us to imagine what it would be like to be in a real relationship. Mundane, suburban togetherness seemed to be a mutual goal of ours.

I think the novelties of this new environment and seemingly "playing house" with Tyler on the weekends gave our second try some new life. It was almost like it was a different set of people trying to make it work in a completely different circumstance, even though it was just a few months after the break up. To be clear, Tyler and I had never made it far enough to be boyfriends. That said, we seemed to be "in like" again and willing to figure things out. I remember on one occasion we were at his house, eating take out. I was emboldened to ask him how he felt about spending time with me this second time around.

A few days prior, Tyler and I had quite a heavy text exchange about where our relationship was going. Tyler, of course, brought up my so-called flakiness factor, in that I left him without much notice for a seemingly small issue. I knew that I had some work to do to convince Tyler I was serious about this second attempt. This exchange ended in a very long paragraph text from me to him. As many of you may know, paragraph texts are never normal and often indicative of convincing, begging, or straight up fact-based arguing. This paragraph text was more of a plea. It was me acknowledging that I really cared for Tyler, and that the way he treated me was rare and amazing and something I really wanted in a life partner. I acknowledged where I went wrong on the past try and why I was perhaps not ready for love on the level that he was so ready to give. I even mentioned that finding issue with the depth of our conversations might have been some cop out to get out of doing the work to make our relationship successful.

I had a tendency to send a lot of paragraph texts in my then-nascent gay dating life. I almost feel like those texts were how I convinced myself of the thoughts I was writing. When you start a paragraph text, you never really know where it's going. It starts with a feeling and then your fingers just vomit it out, like confused poetry generally too dramatic for the situation. Luckily, paragraph texts almost always impressed a guy and got him to soften to my viewpoints. I think this is because they show a depth and effort that is otherwise unseen in gay dating. As someone who has received paragraph texts of my own, I am always impressed when a person has thought of me enough to spend an extra amount of time expressing himself or wanting my attention. Whether or not the situation with the paragraph-sender is right or meant to be, they always seem to buy time.

So, here I was on Tyler's couch, bringing up the paragraph text and asking him where we stood. At first, he brushed off the question. I kept bugging him until he offered an answer. He said that he talked to his best friend in the days after I sent my long "proclamation-of-wanting-to-be-with-him" message. He told me that his friend said that if she had gotten a text like mine from someone from her past, she would definitely give it another shot. Knowing that Tyler held his best friend in very high regard, I knew from this moment that I would be getting a full-fledged chance at being with him again. That fact was likely why Tyler was holding back. He didn't want me to know that I might have been doing things right.

Despite this affirmation from his best friend, Tyler remained very cautious in getting too close too fast. Looking back, I can easily see that Tyler was at a place in his life where he was completely ready to love and cherish the first guy he came across that met his criteria. He was ready to take the rare, gay plunge into a committed relationship, with an eye toward marriage and even a family in the future. I had convinced him that with time, I could be that guy. Now I see that I was probably convincing him of that without the knowledge that I could really be who he wanted. I was just doing what I had to in order to buy more time to see if he was someone *I* wanted. Unfortunately, I was barely sure of whom and what I ultimately wanted in the same ways as Tyler.

Times were overall good and Tyler remained sweet, attentive, and affectionate. Tyler would truly spoil me, making sure I had everything I needed to do my school work – taking the dog out, keeping Starbucks iced coffees in my hand at all times. He liked tending to someone and I liked being tended to. That said, we still had our minor disagreements, testing each other's annoyances and limits.

I remember on one occasion, I didn't want to listen to the music Tyler had playing in his car. A seemingly trivial disagreement, but perhaps my periodic "my way or the highway" attitude struck him the wrong way on this day. He freaked out about how I needed to compromise in a relationship and do things I didn't want to. He was probably the right one on this argument, but I instead became silent and made him pay for it the rest of the day. This, in itself, should have been evidence to Tyler that I might not have been ready for the compromises an adult relationship requires. However, because these disagreements were few and far between, we soldiered on.

What Almost Happens in Vegas

My relationship with Tyler, like others, culminated in the ultimate test for LA gays – can we survive a weekend in Vegas together? I ended up driving and we took my dog with us. We were truly testing the limits of playing house in sin city. Tyler, as he always did, set us up for a very nice weekend. Using his connections, he booked a great hotel that allowed for a typically expensive dog-in-room accommodation. We planned to see a show one of his friends was performing at too.

I remember getting into the room, and as the excitement of what we were doing faded, I found myself lying in bed with Tyler. It was quiet. I wasn't sure what aspect of Vegas or a hotel room heightened the stakes in a relationship. We were doing nothing different than we had done at home. By this point, Tyler and I had become intimate on a couple occasions. It seemed that this moment should have been exciting, but was actually making me feel some pressure. We were "really" doing this – being a couple. This is what I had begged for in my paragraph text and here it was. I distracted myself with the dog and we went down to a restaurant to hang out and plan the rest of our day. It was still quite early on a Saturday so we weren't sure what we were going to do. Our time at the restaurant seemed to lessen my pressure, as it was more of a lunch-type vibe of us sitting at a table talking. Something about that room just made me feel like we were a couple and it was making me nervous.

We decided to spend the rest of our day at the pool. Neither of us realized that a murder would be happening out there. If we did, I think we would have skipped it. That afternoon, on a beautiful 100-degree Vegas afternoon, I silently put a knife through our relationship and Tyler's heart. But, let's back up.

What I now realize I was feeling in the hotel room was a culmination of a lifetime of heteronormativity that had morphed into my own fear and internalized homophobia. I was feeling pressure because I was in a hotel room with a man that I was holding out to be someone I was dating. We were like the other couples happily going to Vegas, but we were different. I was not proud of myself and I was not proud of us. I didn't feel happy like everyone else. I was suddenly overcome with a feeling of shame. I realized that my talk was bigger than my own comfort with my sexuality. I was out here begging for this guy to love me, and I was close to getting my wish before I realized that I wasn't even ready for a blessing like him in my life. These revelations came piece by piece.

As we got ready for the pool, Tyler put on some shorter than usual swim trunks. You know the type - they aren't super short but short enough to say, "I am not the straight bro out here with my girlfriend." I felt that my shorts, while not "bro length," were conveying the message of "I'm not making any statement about my sexuality, but these shorts fit me appropriately without being obnoxiously long." At this age, to look back and think that I was equating the length of swim trunk to how gay or masculine someone appeared to be is disappointing. I know now, of course, that absolutely none of this should matter.

That said, at this time, I felt uncomfortable to be at the pool with Tyler, who I felt appeared obviously gay. With me next to him, this made a statement about my sexuality that I realized in that moment I wasn't prepared to make. I don't know why this was all happening to me in this moment. I had been to dinners and out with Tyler numerous times. I'm sure we appeared to be a couple in many of those situations as well. Perhaps I was fooling myself the entire time in thinking that we just came across as friends. I was not comfortable enough for PDA, so I guess it was plausible for me to think that we looked friendly, not boy-friendly. I'm actually not sure why this logic would not have applied at the Vegas pool. Certainly two heterosexual bros or dads could be at the pool together too. But this time, I felt shame. We went out to the pool and Tyler asked if I wanted to get a drink. I felt some relief as he walked off to get our margaritas. Here I was alone, not making any statement. I was just myself, and this was familiar and comfortable.

It was not long before Tyler came back with our massive Vegas margaritas. He noticed a dramatic shift in my mood and I wasn't sure how I was going to deal with him or the situation. He asked what was wrong. I assured him that nothing was wrong – I was just tired and wanted to relax for a bit. I don't think he bought it, but he gave me some time. We both lounged as Tyler continued to talk and ask me questions. I was so in my head that I wasn't prepared to have a normal conversation with him. The question came up again, "what's wrong?" After a while I became silent. I was completely overwhelmed with my own thoughts. I zoomed out of myself, looking at the situation from above. Here I was with this amazing, sweet guy that was doing so much for me and making a genuine attempt to be a part of my life in a real way. I was so afraid to tell him what I was feeling. The shame that he was making us look gay, the embarrassment and discomfort I felt in portraying that publicly at the pool with a bunch of strangers. I felt sick.

What was happening in this moment was not a creation of Tyler or myself. It was the byproduct of growing up in a time with absolutely no accessible, publicly gay couples or role models on TV, in the movies, and certainly not in my own life. I was coming to terms that I was in fact part of a culture and lifestyle that I was raised to believe was completely taboo. I wasn't brought up very religiously, so I did not feel that this was a sin. I just felt shame that this wasn't normal. It was never something I saw myself sharing with my family or celebrating. I was out to friends at this time but not my family. I reflected upon how you never see a happy gay couple in the Vegas tourism commercials (save for their recent material), just a typically beautiful heterosexual couple. *They* can be proud, *they* can be happy. I was different. I was supposed to live in the shadows. What *I* was doing was wrong and most people at the pool had to feel that way. My lifestyle felt like a losing argument.

Because of my silence, we ended up calling it a day and heading back to the room, with a disappointed Tyler and two barely sipped margaritas. I remained silent and Tyler just watched some TV. I know that he was completely concerned about what I was dealing with. He had no clue. Eventually, I started talking and crying. I explained to him that I was overwhelmed and that I was probably not ready to be in a gay relationship on the level that he was. He was completely surprised and confused about why I had come to this sudden revelation when we were doing nothing new today. In that moment, I couldn't explain to him why this day was different. Looking back, I see that our environment – Vegas – was partially the culprit. This typically unfriendly forum for all types of drunken people to judge one another raised the stakes for me.

To publicly be in love and gay in such a scary and judgmental environment changed things for me. I could never see me proudly holding his hand and walking down the Strip. I felt shame in doing the things and activities so typically associated with heteronormativity and the happy straight couples portrayed by the media. He started crying too, and I completely understood. He probably felt defeated, in that he had put his complete effort and emotions into making it work with me twice, only to be shut down again with no notice. We were in a setting that was probably leading him to imagine how it would be for us when we were officially boyfriends or even married. This was supposed to be a happy, romantic weekend away. Something we were doing for us. I had managed to kill it even before it really started. He understandably became silent and needed some time. We did our own thing and managed to fake it through an awkward dinner by me convincing myself that dinner was something we had done together a million times and ultimately, we needed to eat.

I wasn't mad at Tyler, I was angry with myself and embarrassed that I felt this way. I was concerned that Tyler thought I was leading him on this whole time. I knew that he had lined up for us to go to a Michael Jackson-themed show that his friend was involved in later that evening. I wasn't sure if we would still be going or if I would even have the energy to fake it for the rest of the evening. I knew he would also want to meet up with his friend after the show, who probably knew me to be the guy Tyler was dating.

At dinner, Tyler mentioned that he definitely needed me to keep it together through the show. Despite both of our moods being destroyed, I knew that I owed it to him to make it through the night. It was completely awkward doing yet another "couples activity" after expressing my shame and regret in us even appearing to be a couple. At least I was able to watch the show to distract me. It was particularly poignant to hear Michael Jackson telling me to "start with the man in the mirror," and ask him to "change his ways." I had no idea how or when I would be taking that advice. I awkwardly survived meeting Tyler's friend briefly, skirting any questions about our relationship entirely.

We went to sleep in a room saturated in regret and emotion, waking up early so I could drive him home and we could both move on with our lives. I felt that the night was dragging along as a punishment, so I could marinate in my own shame and misery. We finally made it back to LA. As he got his bag out of the trunk and came to my window, I just remember saying "I'm sorry." Our eyes, locked together, mutually tearing up one last time. I drove off and never saw Tyler again. I had selfishly broken his heart twice just to learn a little more about myself.

[5] WHAT TYLER TAUGHT ME

One of my earlier lessons with Tyler is one that continues to be a recurring problem in my gay dating pursuits. Specifically, I often reflect on that first break up with Tyler when I felt that our mental connection was lacking and that our conversations were becoming boring. Looking back, I know that I should have given Tyler much more leeway and put in significantly more effort in heightening our conversations and connection. As I reflected earlier – there is a difference between not settling and not trying, and I always question which I am doing when it comes to my dating life.

Perhaps one aspect of this is generational for me. As a millennial, I feel that my contemporaries and I are taught that we can attain absolutely anything we want. A professor of mine referred to our generation as conditioned to be "special snowflakes." We are all raised to be completely unique and perfect in our own ways and told that we can do whatever, be whatever, and have whatever. While dramatic, that professor may have been onto something. It's good to be raised to feel special and to be encouraged to have anything you desire, but does that paint a false image of reality? Does that create a generation of people that do not know how to work through situations? A generation of people who would rather quit when things get difficult to find something more "perfect," or easy?

It's tough to know for sure – but now when I feel like I want to walk away from a situation, I always ask myself if I have tried as hard as I want to for this particular guy. My advice is not to torture yourself to make it work with every single person you date, but rather, if you like more aspects of a person than you dislike about them, try your best to work out your differences a few times before writing them off. Do not always count on there being something better or easier around the corner. In my own history, I feel like I have left some pretty awesome guys for trivial issues, and I always wonder what could have been if I had more patience.

Another angle is that of instant gratification. Perhaps it is so easy to find fault with someone because I felt safe in knowing that there were literally 100 guys waiting in line, or on the grid, for me afterward. Typically after a relationship of any seriousness fails, there is a period of mourning. An immediate loss or grief of the aspects of the person that made you happy. Perhaps if a relationship ends on bad terms, there is a euphoria that it is over. But in all cases, there should be a period of reflection, sad or happy, on why things ended and what you take as a lesson out of the situation. This reflection, of course, equips you not to make similar mistakes in the future.

With the advent of Grindr and similar apps, however, this period of reflection is often lost to distraction. So many of us hop right back on the apps immediately after a relationship or dating comes to a conclusion. We talk to someone, anyone, who is remotely attractive and attentive to us. I can think of countless times I've messaged 10 guys back to back just to get anyone to talk to me and fill the void of sadness I felt after a break up, or even after someone I really liked shut me down.

We get into a mindset of making up for the past as quickly as possible. Some may write this off as rebounding, which is nothing new, however, I feel that the Grindr generation takes rebounding to the next level. I consider that with Tyler, the instant gratification of Grindr fueled me to our petty break up, with the knowledge that someone would hold my attention as soon as I left him. The tool or technology of Grindr seems to plant a seed in our minds before our relationships even come to an end. For some, the knowledge that something is around the corner as soon as they want it accelerates the demise of their present relationship. I imagine how it would be if Grindr didn't exist in my first break up with Tyler. Would I have been more motivated to make it work and explore other angles to our issues? Would I have tried harder if I lived in a small town in the 90's and Tyler was the only likable guy for miles? Some have called this the "next-better-best," syndrome – always feeling like there is something better to explore beyond your current situation.

The culture of instant gratification created by Grindr encourages you to endlessly search for hook ups and companionship, but the same culture encourages you to end that companionship when even marginally inconvenient, so you can go back to Grindr and try again. It is a system of cyclical failure, perhaps intentionally created by app developers or perhaps wholly unintentional. Sometimes humanity creates tools and advances for problems that create entirely new problems (see: social media.) I do feel that without the ability to return to apps, I would have had significantly more reflection about my first demise with Tyler. Perhaps it would have been enough reflection to teach me to make better choices with him and many others. I would encourage everyone to keep the effects of instant gratification in mind when it comes to dating, as it may be controlling you more than you think.

My relatively short relationship with Tyler also taught me immensely about my comfort with my sexuality and myself. At this critical mid-point in my coming out journey, I thought I had everything figured out. I was becoming comfortable and confident in being openly gay. I was much less fearful of being caught or judged for who I was and what I was doing. Almost all of my friends knew about my sexuality and were very supportive. I was beginning to speak more freely about opinions I had hidden in the past for fear of giving myself away. Although I was not yet out to my family, I didn't worry about that much. I think the high of coming out to *anyone* lasts you for quite a while before you contemplate any next steps. It was only after Tyler that I felt internalized issues with my sexuality and wondered if, not when, I would ever tell my family. In a sense, I went into my relationship with Tyler completely riding the high of coming out. Nothing can stop me, I thought, I'm fierce and I'm free and I'm *that* bitch and maybe one of you will be on my level if you're lucky. I guess since I had come out, I falsely believed that I no longer had issues to deal with. My months with Tyler shut that concept down.

Although Tyler completely changed my outgoing and even ostentatious approach to gay dating, this shift had absolutely nothing to do with him. Tyler unleashed emotions in me that had probably been lurking for a decade. Tyler was the first guy that was actually good enough to realistically date long term. Despite my minor issues with him, his relative perfection turned the spotlight right back on me. Up until now, the reason I was single was that "no one was good enough." While I was dealing with numerous scrubs, so to speak, I am certain that in retrospect, many of the guys I dated in this period deserved a better shot. I was putting the blame on Tyler and all of the others. "You guys aren't good enough for me," I internally complained. I wish I could tell them all now that I actually wasn't good enough for them. Tyler was doing his part, and I wasn't prepared for that. I wasn't prepared to face the reality of being gay, with someone else, in a loving and permanent relationship.

The internalized shame that Tyler brought out in me during this time can still bring me to tears as I write this. Later in this book, I conjecture that it might take being out for more years than you were closeted for that shame to truly start dissipating, The Vegas trip with Tyler brought out everything I was hiding my whole life. It was those first experiences with Internet pornography - heterosexual pornography – and noticing that I was more focused on the male than the female. There was *years* of that. It was the extremely uncomfortable years in middle and high school, particularly in sports and locker rooms. Being forced into camaraderie with primarily straight boys fully armed with the aggressively anti-gay rhetoric of the

90's and 00's.

It was the number of times the popular middle school boys would call everyone faggot in that locker room before PE. It was the times they would single me and the other apparently weaker, sensitive boys out for that ridicule. It was attempting to change my PE clothes in the blink of an eye, so none of them would tease me for how I looked. It was staring straight ahead at the locker in front of me so none of them would accuse me of watching them change. It was that the cooler boys somehow felt comfortable getting naked and using the rarely-operated showers in that locker room, but that I should feel guilty for having an interest in male nudity, even though I just stared ahead.

How could they be naked around each other, how could they slap each other's asses as a joke, and it be me who was standing in fear of being gay? It was those same cool boys pushing and fighting and physically wrestling with one another. How come when they did things like that it was considered normal, but if I did it, I would immediately brand myself as gay? I continually wondered. It was one of those same boys pinching my ass as I walked to class. Was that a joke, I wondered? Were these boys actually gay? Am I losing my mind? Here I was calculating my every move to avoid being perceived in a certain way, and they could get away with whatever they wanted.

For years I would wonder why I had to fight this perception so hard. Despite all of these steps, was I giving myself away? How could these other boys literally do the gayest things, but it be me who was suffering with my reality? To be clear, those years from middle school to high school were certainly a period of transition. I felt as though I was attracted to girls and perhaps guys. I wasn't sure, and it would take me another decade to figure out. One thing was for sure, I could only cop to liking girls. That was the only option publicly available to me unless I wanted to be bullied for the rest of my education. It was shocking, further, because I had quite a bit of emotional intelligence for my age. I wasn't the nerd and I wasn't cool. I knew exactly what to say and do to play it safely in the middle. To be liked by enough cool people to fly under the radar of being teased. Perhaps it was this hyper-awareness of myself that led me to analyze my behaviors and the perception of my sexuality so critically.

This behavior and suppression continued through high school. Of course, there was the new ammunition of older men, fully having experienced the puberty cycle. Suddenly, I had to be around "real men" every day and further question myself. I had good taste in men then and now. I knew exactly which ones were cute. It always aligned with the ones all the girls also liked. I could never cop to knowing. It was the confident boys who attracted me in high school. The exuberant ones, the popular ones. They were the ones I wanted to be like in so many ways. They were good at sports. They dated pretty girls. They got to hold their hands, and disgustingly make out before class.

I guess I never envied or saw myself doing that with any of the boys. It just wasn't accepted in that high school environment. Perhaps the only gay fantasy that was even plausible at that time was to *be like* the guys I was attracted to, not be with them. It was only after high school that I felt free enough to experiment and act on my sexuality. Perhaps it was the freedom of being at a school away from my childhood social circle. I could experiment and not talk to certain people again, if necessary. The stakes were far lower than high school, where you would see and be subjected to bullying from the same people, day in and out.

At the pool in Vegas with Tyler, these and so many more homosexual suppressions came boiling out. I was finally in a situation, at a pool in public with a beautiful man. The universe was finally opening a door for me to be myself. I felt relatively safe to do so, but then I was suddenly choked by the decades of suppression. As much as I wanted to enjoy the day at the pool with Tyler, it was every demon in my brain that stopped me. It was so many things: the years of straight porn out of fear, clearing my Internet history and cache if I ever dipped into gay porn, being called "faggot" in the middle school locker room, staring straight at the locker ahead, fantasizing about the high school jock, the confusion that women sexually aroused me but men seemed to arouse me more. Perhaps the blood in that latter scenario was accelerated by anxiety and guilt. And that's why I wanted to throw up there with Tyler as he sipped his margarita and looked into my eyes at that mid-point between hope and disappointment. It was the fact that suddenly, in a single moment, everything that had been wrong for so many years needed to be right. In that single moment, I felt the pressure to let go of all of that guilt and shame. I was nowhere near ready.

Tyler taught me that while it is so easy to be critical of others, people are much less likely to be as critical of themselves. I was parading through the gay dating scene with a false bravado. The high of coming out put me in a cloud of false confidence. It led me to believe that everything would be immediately ok as it pertained to my sexuality. For many, coming out is only the beginning of the work you will need to do on accepting yourself. It is opening the garage door and letting air in, but not beginning to clean a labyrinth of junk worthy of a *Hoarders* episode. For a while you're just like – yes honey – AIR and LIGHT. Then you realize, shit, I might want to park some cars in here one day. Tyler taught me that my garage was cluttered as fuck. And it wasn't until him that I knew that I had to do something about it.

After Tyler, I began to do just that. I didn't have a plan or even any example of how to deal with that internalized shame. Perhaps this book can provide some early guidance to others in the same position. My first suggestion is to start putting yourself in situations that would have made you uncomfortable before. Visit the gay part of town, start interacting with queer people. Read queer books and make queer friends. Dip your toes into the waters of being openly gay, but do not pressure yourself into jumping into a relationship you may not be ready for. Hold someone's hand in private. Feel it, embrace it. Do that before you pressure yourself to hold that same hand in public. Use the age of the Internet to your advantage. You have an encyclopedia of experience at your fingertips. Watch videos online; connect on social media with queer people you relate to. I guarantee you that almost any queer person would be receptive to a message from someone seeking advice about their sexuality.

In sum, recognize that coming out is a process, and feelings from your past may spring up on you suddenly, constantly, or not at all. But you should be prepared to do the work, self-exploration, and ultimately the self-love to get you to a place of comfort. That may include counseling, therapy, long talks with friends, and long talks with complete strangers who have been there before. It is a process that will take time.

With Tyler, I tried to jump into a stick shift I didn't know how to drive. I lied just to get the keys and get into the car. I had no idea what to do after that. Unfortunately, I took Tyler for that very bumpy and short ride with me. I wish I didn't and knew to avoid the situation from the beginning. That said, I do believe that we shouldn't live with regrets. I genuinely hope that for even that brief time, I provided some happiness to Tyler and ultimately showed him that he was deserving of a level of love from someone far more comfortable with their sexuality. Ultimately, Tyler was one of the best men I have ever dated and I know he will make someone very happy one day and treat them as they deserve. Ultimately, my experiences with Tyler fueled me to document my feelings in this book, and hopefully it can now help others. Thank you Tyler.

[6] LESSON THREE: WILLIAM

I felt an instant addiction to the newfound attention that Grindr provided. There was no warning or easing in period for its consuming powers. I still wasn't out, and it was unusual for an app to put a spotlight on an aspect of me that never saw the light of day. All of these guys were suddenly talking to me and showing interest in the one part of me I was hesitant to share in my daily life. By pulling my phone out of my pocket, clicking an orange gremlin-looking icon, and waiting for a refresh, I was instantly soothed by attention from one or two new guys each time. Like an addict taking a hit, every use of Grindr pulled me deeper into a dependency on partially clothed gay strangers. I constantly wanted more attention and better versions of it.

These early years coincided with my moving to LA after finishing my undergraduate degree. Although I grew up in Southern California, I had never lived in LA proper and everything about it was new and exciting. The hip places, the foreign streets, the seemingly important people. It was as exciting as New York, but only an hour away. Of course, New York would not align with my fantasy that I was Lauren Conrad glamorously figuring things out in the city, as thoroughly highlighted in the stories preceding.

Around this time, I found myself dealing with demons aside from my sexuality: anxiety and depression were beginning to dominate my daily life. The worst of my battles with these issues took place toward the end of college, but I was still not completely stable in these post-grad years. Although not a story about my depression, I think this is relevant to my addiction to Grindr around this time. Grindr seemed to be a welcome distraction from dealing with any of the other issues potentially contributing to my depression or anxiety. Grindr allowed me to explore an issue that had yet to come to the forefront in my life. It allowed me to discreetly understand my sexuality and talk to people I had never met – I could joke with them, flirt with them, and fight with them. To be clear, my sexuality was about to take center stage in the issues of my life, but at this time, it seemed like a distant problem to explore.

Are You Up?

Many nights I found myself up late talking to the roster of Grindr men living in Downtown LA. It was probably 2 AM when I started chatting with William. To be more exact, a cropped picture of a shirt started chatting with me and I responded. There comes that hour of the night when Grindr conversations fade off and people start falling asleep on you. It was the mutual insomnia between William and I that kept our conversation going until 4 AM. Given his secretive profile picture with very few details, I asked early on for more pictures.

We exchanged more pictures and he was undeniably handsome. I was surprised that he was hiding himself. Thinking back, however, my picture in this Grindr era was cropped as well. I was always willing to send my face as soon as a conversation started, but was afraid of putting it out there for the world to see. It was a very different time when my primary fear was that the other gay guy at Starbucks would see me online and out me to the world. I later became that *very guy* at Starbucks, incessantly refreshing Grindr to see if the cute gay guy waiting in line was available to chat.

Our conversation that evening focused less on William and

much more on me. Who I was, what I did, and what I was looking for on Grindr. He was probably 8 years older than me at this time so I felt somewhat intimidated and excited that he took an interest in me. I had no problem sharing more about myself than he was willing to offer. I figured the topics would even out if the conversation continued.

I remember William asking me for more suggestive pictures that evening and I obliged. What can I say – it was 4 AM and I was enjoying the attention. Of course, I received very little in return from William. You know that feeling when you send someone a pristine, well-lit racy photo and ask for one in return, and they send you a blurry nude from 2003 with that orange timestamp of the date in the corner? That's what I was getting from William that night. It was fine, because I had seen a couple of him. I at least knew he was handsome, and I was willing to submit to his commands that night. Something about an older man and my severe lack of experience at this time gave him a license to take the lead and be unfair. Eventually, we went to sleep and I was satisfied with the excitement of an older, experienced man who seemed to be really into me.

William would be on and off of Grindr, so our conversation the following day was much more sporadic. I would constantly check if his blank profile was adorned with a green "online" light. The much younger me didn't realize that it was a red flag when a man would talk to you nonstop in the middle of the night and pretty much ignore you during the day. I feel inclined to take this opportunity to spell it out for any younger readers: he only cares about you when he's horny! Run!

I suppose it works if you're getting something mutually positive out of it, but I wasn't. It took several days to even get basic details out of William about his life. He was extremely secretive. Typically, I would move on, but based on his pictures and the way he excited me, I was willing to be patient. I figured good things were worth the wait. Another lesson to my readers – that does not hold true on gay dating apps. Being strung along with no positive end result is actually the norm.

I remember I took a sick day from work around this time and spent the day at my building's rooftop pool. I felt very Heidi Montag on those first days in LA, out here on a Wednesday looking glamorous - as if I didn't need a job and wasn't living paycheck to paycheck. Interestingly enough, William was online when I was out at the pool. It was late morning and I figured he was at work. William knew the complex I lived in; I did not know where he lived. The next thing I see is a photo message from William *of me*, on the rooftop pool. I was completely freaked out. It was some sort of long distance paparazzi-type shot but it was definitely me. I started looking around, confused as to where the hell a camera was and whether or not I was safe.

It was then that William revealed he lived in a high rise several blocks away and from a specific angle of his bedroom, and apparently a very intense camera, he could see me on the rooftop. It was definitely the creepiest way to reveal to someone where you lived, but at least I now knew how close he was. I was a bit thrown off as to whether or not to trust William. This act was very in line with something I would imagine an Internet killer to do. I decided to proceed with caution, but I did still want to proceed. I kept talking to William, trying to find out more about him or when we could potentially meet. He maintained his overall secrecy and would delay the topic of meeting. As long as I was sending him pictures, I was keeping his attention. We weren't moving forward or backward. I was just maintaining whatever this was – an online attraction to a seemingly hot, slightly creepy older man a few blocks away.

One Audi, That's It?

Days later came a shift in my relationship with William. I remember talking to him about the car he drove, and how my car was faster. This seemed to aggravate his ego. He kept insisting that his car was faster, but it was a simple fact that the engine in my car was bigger.

Noticing that this was bothering him, I kept pushing the point. He was becoming upset. I remember thinking – who the fuck cares, they're just cars. But in superficial LA, they were status symbols. He was clearly upset that I had the impression that I had a better car, so he said, "that's not even my real car." I asked him what he meant. He said, "that's my grocery getter." The slow car I was making fun of was apparently his day-to-day car that he didn't mind getting scratched. Mind you, it was an Audi so the statement in itself was ostentatious LA bullshit.

I said it was pretty convenient for him to bring this up now that he was bothered, how did I know he wasn't lying? Out of nowhere, he exploded. He revealed that he was lying to me about everything so far. His measly Audi that I was criticizing was one of five elite luxury cars he was now claiming to have. He said he had a Lamborghini, as well. He said he was not fully out so he had to hide his identity online. He told me he came from money and was well-known, so he couldn't risk being out, especially as a Grindr user. I was shocked and unsure what to believe. Typically, this would sound far-fetched, but we were in LA. It was entirely possible. I asked for a real face picture, by now realizing that the handsome guy in the photos was likely not him.

Those of you who have used Grindr have probably been catfished before. Even if it has happened to you multiple times, it is never less jarring. You typically have invested quite a bit of time and emotion into your catfisher; building an image of them in your head based on the facts and photos they have shared. Even after they admit to lying, there is a brief moment of hope. A moment where you are still trying to defend the idea of them that you built in your head. "Well, maybe he had a good reason for lying," I thought. Maybe I will still be attracted to the real him. I can't relate to the fear of people only wanting me for my money or status, so in a way it's respectable that he didn't lead with it. I didn't care about his money either; I just wanted to meet this guy I had become attached to. Now the mystery had exploded.

Despite these feelings, I was messaging him my frustration and anger with being lied to. I remember begging over and over for his real picture or threatening to block him. That's the only power I had over the situation – removing myself from it. He finally sent a real picture. It was low quality but revealed enough to solidify that he looked very different than the fake photos he sent. It wasn't even the same genre of guy – which I guess is asking a lot for a catfish to be somewhat realistic. I was not attracted to the photo of the "real" him. I didn't know what to do. My couple weeks of complete excitement and damn near obsession with this guy were crushed. I wasn't sure of the right way to proceed. I could be upset, I could just tell him the truth, or I could also lead him on and still act interested to keep the attention going.

I decided to tell him he was not my type. This went as well as it always does on Grindr. Don't get me wrong; you get the occasional guy that is totally respectful that people have different types. But more often, you get someone who is going to blow up on you and cuss you out for being shallow or question you on what specific aspect of him is not attractive. The problem I had with William blowing up on me is that he had this coming. You can't send a fake picture of yourself and then get mad when someone is not attracted to the real you. That is the one situation where you are pretty much asking for it.

He called me shallow because I wasn't willing to accept the real him. I did not see or appreciate his logic or accusation. He was trying to turn the situation against me. If this happened to me today, I would have a calm and rational explanation and be able to move on with no issue. Back then, I felt attacked and was unwilling to let the situation go without feeling like I had won. "I don't like you and you need to understand why I would feel that way," I kept saying. The fight continued to go nowhere until we stopped talking. Neither one of us blocked the other.

It's interesting how being mad at someone but needing their continued attention can be bifurcated in your mind. Like "hey, I absolutely hate you for what you did to me, but unfortunately you were my only source of attention and happiness so if you also take that away you effectively hurt me double." I decided that I wasn't going to allow William to do that to me. I decided that he and I were going to continue talking. Yes - that was the horrible solution I came up with to supposedly punish William for catfishing me.

During this time, I did a lot of self-exploration on why exactly I wanted to keep talking to William. If I wasn't attracted to him, was it because of the allure, the excitement of talking to someone rich and important? Was it to keep the attention going? Was I still curious about the intense sexual chemistry I had built in my head? And did I not care which of his face pictures was orchestrating that chemistry? I really wasn't sure. But the bond was there and I apparently was not willing to let it go just yet. The bottom line for me seemed to be that he had taken up this much of my time, and I wasn't going to let him get the best of me. At the least, I wanted to meet him to confirm whether or not all of these alternative facts that he had provided were true. Perhaps it would be the ultimate revenge and closure for me to find out that he was some habitually lying loser.

Moving On Up

I eventually agreed to go over to his condo. I walked the few blocks. I was completely nervous. Unfortunately, since I was hiding my sexuality at this time, I didn't even make the wise decision of telling anyone where I was going. Kids – even if you are not out, please lie to your friends about why you're going somewhere, but *do* tell them where you are going. I say this because I went to go meet William knowing he already had these weird stalker tendencies and had completely lied to me about who he was. How did I know he wasn't still lying and going to kill me? The early Grindr days were consistently sketchy in this way.

Nonetheless, I showed up at his fancy building. In fact, it was too fancy for me to feel comfortable. The people who lived here had real money. Celebrities, doctors, and lawyers lived here. I was afraid to even walk into the lobby because I knew I looked like I didn't belong. I texted him and he told me he would have security buzz me up. I wasn't that stupid. I told him he would need to come downstairs and show his face in the lobby, with the benefit of people around us, or I would just walk home. For all I know he was scoping me with his telegraphic lens on the sidewalk from above. I waited outside, constantly looking behind my back, essentially waiting to be killed. It was probably 10 PM, and this was years before Downtown LA was actually cool to walk around late at night.

He came outside sloppily dressed in a hoodie and ill-fitting jeans. He was the guy from the second photo, the photo of the catfish. I was not attracted to him, but here I was. He gave me a half-assed, unsatisfying hug (not that I wanted one at all) and asked if I was coming upstairs. He smelled like too much cologne. Like those people everyone knows are wearing too much cologne but no one in life has said anything to them for like 30 years. And I wasn't going to help him out either. I had no idea how to deal with the situation, other than to proceed. So I went up.

In the elevator, I noted that he wasn't as creepy as I thought, and I could tell that this was awkward for him too. That's probably why I felt somewhat safe going inside. They say that talking online is nothing like talking in person – and this was a true exemplification. He was no longer this sexy, mysterious older man. I was no longer willing to submit to his desires. He was just an awkward, apparently rich, often horny guy who lied about himself. And I was a gorgeous, innocent…. ok, fine. And I was scared and reluctant! The elevator took us up to the highest floor in the building. We were probably 30 or 40 stories up. We walked down a deserted hall and it felt like no one really lived here. He finally zeroed in on a door and opened it for me to walk in first.

I was instantly in awe of the city lights from his condo. He had an amazing view of Downtown LA. Furthermore, despite his poor fashion choices, the condo was impeccably decorated. Clearly someone helped him out. Everything felt brand new and expensive. I had never been in a place like this. The place had floor to ceiling panoramic windows, and I remember walking right up to the edge of his apartment. I looked out to the side to see if and how he was able to photograph me at the pool that day. He knew what I was doing, and pointed out where the pool was. He even showed me the camera he used, which had the most intense paparazzi-length lens on it. I asked why he had something like that. He said he was into photography. "And stalking," I thought to myself.

I sat on his couch and examined my surroundings. There's always that moment of reflection when you first enter the personal space of someone you've been talking to. What do I recognize, what do I like? You check what items you may have in common or where you can find connections. Like hey! I like that magazine, or nice Ikea pillows. Nothing in there was from Ikea, though. I did feel like the place was strangely clean. I'm sure he had a cleaning person. I was getting Patrick Bateman vibes. I remember he showed me an unfinished painting on the wall. He said he was painting it. It was of Paris Hilton. I thought it was neither good nor bad. I actually found it striking that he was showing me a human side of him – that he was creative and painted. It was kind of sad that this human side of him manifested in a painting of one of the most vain celebrity figures of the time. Like really? Of all things to paint for your wall, you chose Paris Hilton?

He offered me a drink and I quickly declined. I wasn't interested in potentially getting drugged tonight. Kids – don't accept drinks from Grindr men you just met, please! Instead, he poured one for himself and we sat on his perfectly white couches. I tried to make things less awkward by asking about the view or things around the house. "Oh that's a pretty sculpture, what street is that down there?" It was a very uncomfortable few moments. It was going to continue like this unless I let my guard down. This tended to happen with me on most dates, despite to peculiarity of this one. Meeting in person was never as fluid as the conversation online. It always turned into an awkward question and answer period while you figure out if this is the same person you've been talking to this whole time and if you even enjoy them in human form. He wasn't giving me much to work with.

He wasn't the worst at conversation, but he wasn't necessarily funny or witty. He was kind of boring. After a while, I could sense that he wanted to salvage the night by turning it into a hook up. Since talking wasn't working, I suppose he figured we could take our clothes off and bond on pretty much the one thing that kept our online conversation going post-catfish revelation. He asked if I wanted to go into his room. I declined. I think I was beginning to realize that I liked almost nothing about him, and I should have known this from the moment he revealed he was lying. Why did I have to take it this far? Why am I in his condo? I should have snapped into my senses when he came down and met me in the lobby. I should have walked away. Now I have to figure out how to leave without it being awkward or without him potentially getting mad and killing me.

We talked a bit longer and I told him I was getting tired and should probably go. He asked if I was sure. I said yes. He asked if I wanted to just spend the night with him instead of walk home this late. I told him I'd be fine, and it was only a few blocks. In reality, I didn't know if it was more dangerous to brave the streets of Downtown at this hour or to brave the sheets of downtown at this hour. To be mugged or wake up next to his mug, that was the question. The answer was not hard. At least on the streets I could run for my life. In here, I was trapped. He seemed disappointed, but let me go with relative ease. That made me feel better. I rode down the hotel-caliber elevator alone, and walked out of the lobby. I wonder how many times this security guard saw innocent young gay men leave this building alone at this hour. I wanted to say, "this isn't a walk of shame honey, this is a walk of virtue."

I made it back home and was never so relieved to be back in my comparatively humble surroundings. Grind is a fucking trip, I thought. It can flip your surroundings and safety upside down in a matter of minutes. I didn't want to talk to or hear from William again. I blocked him in every way I knew how and pretended the whole thing never happened. I was sad for a while, mostly from the lack of attention and not having that go-to person to talk to, but I got over it fairly quickly.

Third Chances

Of course, in gay dating, nothing is ever officially over the first time you think it is. I always wondered why this was. Why do we continue going back? Perhaps because there are so few guys to begin with. With a small supply of men, it's necessary that we thoroughly torture ourselves by exploring every crevice of the opportunities that come our way. It's like the hidden meat in the extremities of a lobster. It is hard to get to and there's not much reward, but you might as well since you already paid for it. I also wonder if this is only the case with guys that we deem to be of a certain quality or caliber. For instance, I find that in the LA dating scene, there is a very small subcategory of guys who have good jobs, don't need to be at the clubs every night, and are somewhat eligible to take home to mom. Those guys tend to be given more chances than one because they are seemingly aligned with my personal desires. Even if it doesn't work out the first couple of times, we might give each other another shot on a subsequent dating app encounter.

You figure, hey, that little drama we had was a year ago and no one better has come along, and he was pretty good at X, Y, or Z, so why the hell not? But that doesn't always seem to be the case with guys who we may be using for a limited purpose. For instance, the guys who we think are too young and would never work for dating, but are serviceable for a hook up. I don't find myself going back to these "limited purpose guys" or even thinking about them again in the future. Finally, it could be the universal concept that it's easier to remember the good times and forget the bad. While not unique to gay people, I think we deal with such bullshit and trash on dating apps that the few guys who can hold a conversation or did something thoughtful in the past are looked back on very fondly.

I think that a combination of those factors led me to talk to William again. It was no more than a few months after the encounter at his condo. I had probably gone through a blocking and hating my life cycle on Grindr, leading me to delete the app and start back over. As many of you know, when you do that, all of your prior blocks are erased and you're suddenly faced with the many, many profiles of your past. Like, oh yeah, I forgot that my next-door neighbor was into S&M - I blocked him a good year ago. Similarly, a few blocks away, there was William again. With the benefit of months of silence, it was easy to remember him fondly. The good times came back swiftly. The attention, in particular, that he provided was something that I was devoid of for these months in between.

"Who cares if I wasn't attracted to him," I thought. Maybe I didn't even give him a fair shot. Maybe I was so mad about the catfishing that we didn't have a proper chance to get to know one another. This is a dangerous line of reasoning that was recurrent for me in gay dating. Since a majority of my dating interactions were very short before something went wrong, I always had that excuse in my back pocket. "Maybe he didn't have enough time to show me who he was-- maybe I was too hard on him." In reality, most of the men I thought back on using this "maybe" line of reasoning had clearly proven their character to me. William, especially, had shown his true colors. At the end of the day, he catfished me, and I'm not convinced that catfishing requires forgiveness.

Nonetheless, nothing better had come along and here he was. So, I messaged him. He quickly responded. I couldn't say I was surprised since things ended on my terms. The problem was, he didn't seem thrilled to hear from me. I guess it was easy to forget that I left his house, went home, and completely deleted him from my life without warning. Sure, the awkward condo interaction should have been a clue to him, but I guess he was right to be upset since I was the one messaging him again. I was acting as if he was disposable and I could use him whenever I wanted, without consequence or explanation for my prior actions.

We went back and forth for a bit before he accused me of being mentally unstable. I was shocked by his accusations, but I saw where they were coming from. I recalled that in our many late nights of messaging, I opened up to him about the depression I was going through at the time. He seemed to be helpful in those moments and talked to me about similar issues he had faced. Now, it seemed, he was throwing this back in my face by saying the reason I was distant and dropped him so easily was that I was depressed and aloof. He accused me of using him the whole time for attention and never really caring about him at all. I responded with an equal accusation that he was using me as some younger sexual conquest. Clearly, I said, he couldn't get someone his own age or at his level to date him seriously, so he had to impress younger men with what he had and that's how he got them to sleep with him. I pointed out that his strategy didn't ultimately work on me, and that's why he was upset. We continued and argued, and neither of our positions were getting us any further or making us happier.

"What is the end game?" I asked him. We can either block each other again and move on, or figure this out. I suggested that since it seemed to be worth both of our time to fight with each other, we clearly had some interest in the other person to care about their opinion. How romantic, right? I was basically saying that you're good enough to fight with so maybe you could be good enough to date. And with that logic, we decided to give it another try. I suggested that since our prior efforts were largely based on sexually messaging in the shadows of the downtown night, maybe we could try something new. Maybe if we went on a real date – a dinner – we could get to know each other as real humans and see if we had a connection. He surprisingly agreed. I could tell that a part of him was tired of living in the Grindr shadows. He was actually more open with his sexuality than I assumed. He seemed to be out to some friends, but not at work or in the public. That's why he couldn't risk being identified using Grindr. It would out him to a level he wasn't comfortable with. But he was comfortable enough to publicly go to a dinner with me, where we would undoubtedly appear to be on a date together.

Barbeque and BMW's

Days later, he picked me up in a 3-series BMW. One of the grocery-getter cars, I joked. He noted that he had traded in the Audi I made fun of months ago. I genuinely wondered if it got traded in because I made fun of it. How LA. He was wearing a nice button up shirt. I remember thinking – wow, he's trying. I didn't dress as nicely as I usually would for a date. Despite being the one who had reached back out to him, I felt that I had more leverage than him, and that he wanted this more than me. Therefore, I could wear whatever the hell I wanted to. We drove a few miles to go to his favorite Korean barbeque spot. I was a fan of LA's KBBQ scene, so I was comforted that at least the food would be good. It was strange to be hanging out with William in public. It was in such contrast to the way we met. Here we were, holding ourselves out as each other's dinner date. I remember still feeling uncomfortable with my level of attraction to him, or lack thereof. I figured that I needed to give it some time to see how our personalities connected.

He ordered a beer and I had water. I needed to be clear-minded for this investigation. The dinner went fairly well. We talked about life, and the difficulties of the dating scene. He joked that his friends pegged him as having a type. "The cross fit and day party boys," he laughed. I remember thinking I was nothing of the sort. It actually highlighted his dating priorities to me – beauty and fun. It was clear that I was seeking a much deeper connection than William was. From his anecdotes of partying all over LA, and dropping the names of the venues and people he was hanging out with, I knew that William was quite "into the scene." He placed importance on where he was going, what he was doing, and who saw him doing it. I, on the other hand, was all about whom I was doing all of those things with. I could care less about what we were doing, I just wanted to find a person that I connected with deeply. Mentally and physically, a quality connection was ultimately my priority - even in those early Grindr years. Despite the excitement of trading suggestive pictures, I learned early on that hooking up with strangers made me feel empty.

I continued to give William time through the date to show me another side of him. I knew that I had a tendency to write people off or run away. I recognized that dates could be more uncomfortable to others than they were for me. I knew that it was hard for people to instantly open up about deep topics, whereas I could often jump into them. Our dinner wrapped up and William asked if I wanted to hang out at his place for a bit. Having already braved the tense initial hang out at his place, I didn't mind spending more time with him. I had a roommate anyway, so this seemed to be the only viable option since I wasn't about to go clubbing with the guy.

I remember him driving into his parking structure, a part of the complex I had not seen before. My jaw dropped. I had never seen so many Bentley's and Range Rovers. He knew by now that I liked cars so he began pointing out the notable ones. "That one is pretty rare, that one belongs to so and so." Let's just say that certain reality show personalities owned some of these vehicles. I was beginning to get a sense that this guy was not lying about how rich he was. We turned and turned and made our way to his parking spaces.

Suddenly I saw myself looking straight at a Lamborghini. "There it is," he said. I was both in awe of the vehicle and also at the fact that he wasn't lying about owning it. I always kind of questioned if what he had said during that catfish revelation didn't border on hyperbole. He parked what now was confirmed to be the measly BMW we were riding in. We got out and he started walking toward the elevators. All I could do was look at his cars. He noticed and asked if I wanted to hear the engine. I had never been this close to a Lamborghini before. He started it up and the engine revs were instantly magnified by the fact that we were in an enclosed garage. I remember thinking, if only he was as impressive as this fucking car.

We got into his condo and sat down on the same couches that we so uncomfortably rested on months before. I never thought I would be back in this space or situation. I felt much more comfortable this time, having seen a more human side to William. That being said, this date didn't give me anything new to cling to as far as hope for our compatibility. I could see, however, that William was much more relaxed and carefree this time around. I felt like he had put himself out there and definitely thought that it was working. He was probably thinking that I was into it. Soon enough, however, we were in the same situation as before. I tensed up being in his space because I felt that the pressure was on to hook up. Especially now that he had bought me dinner. I remember noticing that the restaurant we ate at actually had a B rating from the health department. It was a nice and very busy restaurant, but for whatever reason it had a B. I thought, wow - if he expects me to put out for a grade-B KBBQ joint, he is delusional.

He offered for us to watch a movie on his couch and cuddle. This was a convenient gay euphemism for two hours of foreplay before you ultimately have to put out, since you refuse to do so now. I rejected that as well. I could tell he was getting impatient and I was beginning to feel a little guilty. I knew that the longer I stayed, the more I was leading him on. I guessed that by this part of the date, his regular cross fit and day party boys would be impressed by his lifestyle. But I knew those types of boys, and I knew that they were probably the most shallow in LA. They didn't like him for his looks, that was for sure. They liked him for what he had and under the premise that he would float their lifestyle for a while. They could take glamorous Instagram selfies with his pool and cars, and hope that he didn't ask to be in the photos. In fact, they would have a built in safety mechanism in that he didn't want to be identified as gay anyway. But one thing is for sure, they would put out sexually at this point to keep the odds of using William in their favor.

This night confirmed to me what I knew long ago…I was not like those guys. From the very moment William shared a real photo of himself, I honestly told him that he was not my type. The first time I met him, it seemed to be out of pure curiosity. To confirm what he lied about and what he didn't. To see if I could continue milking him for attention despite not being attracted to him. This second time seemed to be out of selfishness. No one had captured my attention quite the way that he did when we first met. I convinced myself that he was worth a second shot and that the initial excitement would come back. I tried to find redeeming qualities in him, and I did find some. But I realized that attraction was critical, and I had absolutely none for William. It didn't help that our personalities and interests didn't align either.

I told William that I needed some time to think about everything, and had to go. He asked why, and if I was sure. I told him I just needed to think – nothing was wrong. He offered to drive me home and I told him I would walk. I went down the elevator and walked past that same security guard. I wondered if he thought I couldn't get enough the first time around? I wanted to say, "honey this is a walk *confirming* the virtues I displayed the first time I walked out of here." I went home and texted William to thank him for the night, but tell him that I didn't think we had anything in common. He was upset. I attribute this to the entitlement of growing up privileged. I was probably one of the few people in his life who told him "no," and who was not ultimately swayed by what he had. I felt shallow for even having tried again. I wondered if I would have done the same for anyone else, or if I had fallen victim to the allure of his lifestyle. Nonetheless, I was proud that I didn't ultimately give in to what he wanted.

Despite this closure on my end, this would not be my last encounter with William. It would be about two years later that William told me he was planning to kill me, texting me consistent confirmations of his threats. These threats arose soon after William began seeing another guy from my past. I am eager to discuss the entire ordeal in a future installment of *The Grid*.

[7] WHAT WILLIAM TAUGHT ME

As one of my earlier memories of a tangible Grindr relationship, William taught me quite a bit about my desires and motivations in the newfound world of gay dating. William strangely resulted in a questioning of my own ethics and values. That's probably rare for your typical Grindr interaction. I was constantly questioning why I continued to talk to him for as long as I did. It was clear to me that I didn't have a physical attraction to him, so what was I trying to gain?

I asked myself over and over again whether or not it was my perception that William was ultra-wealthy or important that gave him a hold over me. Many of us are shallower in our formative years, so I don't doubt that some of his wealth or perceived power attracted me to him. I think the fact that he was quite a bit older and seemingly more experienced than me conspired with his wealth and power. He was an intriguing mystery. I often thought of what my life would be like if I dated him. Suddenly I would find myself at LA parties and events in the scene. Would I be living that coveted lifestyle as portrayed on *The Hills* with William? Quite possibly.

Another consideration with William was the fact that I viewed his success as potentially legitimatizing a lifestyle that I had a lot of guilt about. I had yet to come out at this time and, like many of us, I had a fear of the repercussions of doing so. I felt like my world may come crumbling down around me after coming out. I was nervous that my parents would not accept me. I was nervous that my friends, although enlightened and supportive, might feel that I had been lying to them about my sexuality for quite some time. I knew that there had been rumors or discussion about it in the past. I worried that I would lose the comforts and support that I had grown accustomed to in my two short decades of life. William, however, was a hope for stability. Not that we made it very far, but I imagined that if I dated him, it wouldn't matter what others thought of me. Essentially, I felt that my "choice" of being gay would be perceived by the world as a good call because I had the love and support of a wealthy, smart, and successful gay man. People could think what they wanted, but my potential lifestyle with William would shut them up.

This last point is something I often think about. When seeking partners, I often wonder what my motivations are in finding someone. Many of us logically seek a partner who might have similar values, habits, preferences, and goals. For instance, if you work a corporate job, you may seek someone with a similar job or hours. If you have a PhD, your partner's education level may be important in determining long-term compatibility. If you're a successful actor, you may want to find a partner who has relative success in his own vocation, so you won't have any fear of being used as a come up. Those are the logical motivations behind finding a partner "on the same page" as you, so to speak. But could there be a deeper reason?

Could it be that we are looking to find a partner who legitimizes a lifestyle that we have lingering guilt about? In dating, I often met men who ultimately made me feel that they liked me for my accolades or accomplishments, rather than my personality. For instance, some may find it desirable to tell their parents that they are dating a lawyer or doctor. Jobs that are viewed as conventionally "successful" may ease the lingering discomfort or pain their parents have because their child is gay. "Well, he may be gay, but at least he married a doctor." I actually had a guy tell me that he was tired of the gay dating scene because everyone on the apps was a waiter or aspiring actor and they weren't good enough to be a part of his life, since he had a Master's degree. That makes me wonder — are we being picky due to our own standards and priorities or are we compensating for underlying guilt? It may be that since we identify as queer, we feel the need to be twice as impressive to prove to the unaccepting world that our choices are valid and worthy.

My experiences with William also forced me to consider my sexual desires, and the guilt surrounding them. Many of us may have felt a lot of guilt during or after our first gay sexual encounters. For me, my first encounter was a culmination of years of thoughts and fantasies about men that I felt were forbidden and wrong, in so many ways. After that first encounter, I was overwhelmed with feelings of failure and disappointment in myself. I couldn't look in the mirror. I couldn't look my parents in the eyes when I spoke to them for quite a while. I felt like I gave in to something evil, and there could be no redemption for me. Before Grindr, it was pretty difficult to meet men to even act on these sexual desires while in the closet. But with Grindr, these opportunities — and the associated guilt - were suddenly recurrent.

Overnight, it wasn't the sporadic evil gay sex encounter I was facing. Rather, it was the hundreds of opportunities for this so-called evil sex, every day. Although I never even slept with William, he forced me to consider these feelings of guilt in relation to gay sexual desire. I sent William many suggestive photos, and even videos as he requested it. In a way, it felt good and liberating to be able to trust someone and explore this side of myself. Perhaps the fact that he was older made me feel as though he was leading the way on a path that I was far too scared to illuminate myself. But every time I sent William a photo or video that he wanted, I felt tremendous guilt. It's like I was building a digital paper trail of sin. Every time I pressed send, I took one step further into this unknown trail. I didn't really fear that my pictures would leak or even cause me to be outed, as I was careful not to include my face in them. What these exchanges with William solidified was that I was going further in a direction that I felt might be wrong.

I carried that fear and guilt for many years. In many ways, it is an issue I still deal with and need to work on in my current life. I trust and hope that there will be a tipping point. A point at which the years of guilt and shame surrounding being gay will be outweighed by the years of freedom and happiness I have felt as an openly gay man. Since I have fewer years as out and happy, I suppose it makes sense that I still have to work on the remnants of shame regarding gay sexual desire in my life.

The only advice I can really give to readers here is to affirm that gay sex and physical desire are not wrong in any way. It is completely natural and beautiful to want to explore intimacy with someone of the same sex. It will likely feel weird and confusing in the early years, but it gets better. For me, this is something I learned once I got into more committed relationships as opposed to hook ups. With time, you too will become intimate with people who you are more comfortable with, and you will also grow more comfortable with yourself. When you begin to have intimate experiences with people you trust and love, people who are patient and caring, you will likely have a renewed and positive outlook on sex. Unfortunately, the early experiences can be awkward, especially for the many young men who turn to apps to find them. Just be patient and safe, and know that things will improve if you deal with sexual guilt.

Furthermore, do not feel guilt or shame if you choose to privately exchange nude photos with other consenting adults. Be smart about it, but do not feel guilty. At the end of the day, it is a human desire and sending nudes is often a more responsible way to handle a human need than sleeping around with everyone on your grid. Maybe just crop your face out before doing so!

Aside from issues of guilt are the issues of safety that William presented. Although we didn't have sex, he pushed me to make choices that often went against my gut instincts. Many of us can agree that when we are driven by sexual arousal, we make decisions that we come to regret. I constantly felt this way with William. There were numerous red flags that should have cautioned me to potentially dangerous future situations.

For instance, the fact that he admitted to catfishing me showed me the ease with which he could lie. On one hand, I feel sympathy for catfishers, especially when they are hiding some physical trait that society has deemed as undesirable. Everyone deserves love and attention, and perhaps catfishing is the only quick way for some people to receive it. That said, when someone online shows to you that they are willing to lie and string you along, you should have no reason to believe them from that point on. The fact that I continued to talk to William is probably why there are like ten seasons of MTV's *Catfish*. We all make bad choices. I may be biased, but I think the questionability of those choices is taken to a new level when it comes to gay men. It should have been another red flag to me when William essentially scoped me out from blocks away using a telegraphic photography lens. His behavior was creepy stalker 101. What did I do? Reclassify his lying and stalking tendencies as mysterious and exciting. I basically walked into an unknown room, with a sign on the door marked "bitch, danger." In this case, it was an unmarked condo.

While I survived unscathed from these run-ins with William, I hope that others can learn from what I went through. Too many gay men have suffered violence and abuse in many situations that start out with the same sexual intrigue that William lured me into. Indeed, gay men have been killed from interactions beginning on Grindr, with people who lie about their identity or who have intentions different from those that they express on the app. It is cliché but completely true that *anyone* can say *anything* online.

Unfortunately, we live in a time where you should treat everything as a potential lie. It is dangerous to allow sexual desire to lessen your focus on safety. To that end, please take the steps necessary to protect yourself before sexual desire takes over and you make potentially dangerous choices. Share your GPS with your close friends at all times. It may be awkward to tell them about all of your dick appointments, but when they constantly know your whereabouts, they can check on you in the event of an emergency. Meet people in public places. So many men on Grindr have hesitated to meet me at a Starbucks. I never meet with those men. If they have something to hide in public, why should they be trusted with a sexual encounter that puts my life and sexual health at risk?

Finally, please be mindful to protect your sexual health in all encounters online. Anyone can say anything about their STI status, but absent being tested with them, you are taking them at their word – which is often meaningless. The best way to stay safe is to protect yourself. Do not let men intimidate you into sexual encounters that are unprotected. It may seem exciting or harmless at the time, but one choice made in the middle of the night on Grindr can have impacts that last a lifetime.

[8] CONCLUSION: ADDICTION

It's scary to take stock of how addicted we have become to Grindr over the years. Let's look at a typical Grindr day. Wake up, check Grindr. Send a few messages out of morning desperation. Check back several more times as you're getting ready for work to see if any of those morning messages hit. Drive to work. Open Grindr at some point in case the man of your dreams is online along your commute. Those are always exciting messages to get, the mysteriously "perfect" men with stats to drool over that were just outside of your local grid at home.

Get to work. Open up Grindr to see if any of those commute log-ins led to a fresh new man messaging you. Log on a couple more times before lunch to maintain any of today's conversations (not to mention those from previous days). Walk to lunch. Open up Grindr to get a fresh batch of men you would not have otherwise picked up across the street. This refresh is usually fruitless, so you go back to work.

The afternoon is a lot like the morning, checking the app out of sheer boredom and desperation. By this point in the day, Grindr has likely drained half of your phone battery. The end of the afternoon gets a bit more frantic as you are trying to find a potential meet up on your way out of work before heading home. Don't get me wrong, "meet up" doesn't mean sex for everyone. It could mean a coffee date, as long as a man shows up. Not finding any viable options by this point in the day becomes very frustrating.

The evening commute is similar to the morning. You're just holding out for someone fresh before you get home and hit your local grid of guys. And then it happens. You're home and you fire up Grindr. There are your four weird neighbors. The images of their torsos are burned into your psyche.

The rest of the night might be a Grindr-per-hour check. This is buttressed by the excitement of actually being able to meet up with someone if you really wanted to during these hours. Most of the time you're just chatting because everyone is generally too lazy to meet up. The guys that are interested in meeting up instantly are usually the sketchiest. The most enticing guys might be the ones who are visiting on business or something and seem legitimate, but only have a limited amount of time. You might go the gym at some point and of course open up Grindr before you walk in to know who to look out for (good and bad) already inside.

There you have it, in a typical day you've been completely addicted to an app full of men who generally drain you of happiness, energy, and hope. You're not sure why you fall into this pattern day in and day out, but the familiarity of it likely gives you a false sense of potential. You know it sucks, but it is still better than nothing at all. You'll wake up tomorrow and do it again.

It is this pattern of addiction to Grindr and similar apps that inspired me to write this book. I started noticing that I turned into a person who I didn't necessarily like, and I attribute much of it to how I have allowed Grindr and other apps to influence my behaviors. In the introduction of this book, I noted that the men of Grindr had slowly ruined me. I had become a shell of the person I originally was. In writing these stories, however, I tried to take responsibility for my own actions in an attempt to understand what part I had in "ruining" myself.

I hope that my discussions of these three men and the lessons I learned have been entertaining, informative, and cautionary. If I can prevent one person from making many of the mistakes I have made, this book will have been worth it. If I can help someone connect the dots and learn something about themselves, this book will have been worth it. If, at the very least, I made you chuckle once, this book will have been worth it. I never wanted to write a book about dating tips or advice. Who am I to tell you how to date successfully? I'm writing this single as hell with my Boston Terrier snoring beside me. What I do have, however, is a lot of experience at failure. It is these stories and experiences of Grindr failures that I felt must be shared with my community. The most memorable tips and lessons come from mistakes.

With time, I hope that more queer people will become cognizant of how apps can change who we are. I hope that more queer people begin to take the steps necessary to reverse some of the damage. This book has been therapeutic for me to write. I now understand how some of my early Grindr relationships impacted me, and how I no longer need to hold on to some of those experiences as baggage. If more of us took that hard look at our pasts, we may just be a nicer and more understanding bunch to date.

CLOSING NOTE

I fully apologize for the cliffhanger I ended the William story with. As a virgin author, I couldn't help myself. I clearly live for the drama. That said, I am optimistic that I will write a second part to *The Grid*, which will pick up on William and discuss three more lessons from the many men of Grindr who have shaped my life. I hope that you will all rejoin me for that journey.

ABOUT THE AUTHOR

Lex, Esq. is an attorney and blogger born and raised in Southern California. He began his blog The Problem Gays as a passion project to freely discuss LGBTQ+ topics and better connect with his community. *The Grid* is Lex's first book and foray into a long-form exploration of the issues he discusses online.

Despite his ongoing efforts, Lex remains single at the time of publication.